China's Korean Minority

About the Book and Author

The record of Korean education in the People's Republic of China reflects a complex relationship between Korean identity and China's shifting minority policy. In general, the Koreans have made a determined, though sometimes tortuous, effort to pursue their own ethnically based educational goals amidst the subtle, at times forceful, pressure for assimilation into the dominant Han culture of China. It is widely believed that among China's fifty-five minority nationalities the Koreans have managed to maintain the highest level of educational achievement while sustaining a strong sense of ethnic identity. This belief is borne out in the successful model for minority education found in the Yanbian Korean Autonomous Prefecture of Jilin Province.

This unique study highlights the development of ethnically based education for the Korean minority in China. With special emphasis on the Yanbian Prefecture, the author explores a set of interrelated questions: Why do Koreans pay so much attention to their own educational programs, especially ethnically oriented ones? How do they manage the challenges and opportunities of ethnic education in the context of China's changing political dynamics? What problems do they encounter in their search for educational excellence? And how effective is the Korean model for ethnic education in China? In answering these questions, the author addresses the issues of educational and cultural autonomy as vital aspects of China's minority policy.

Chae-Jin Lee is professor of political science and East Asian languages and cultures at the University of Kansas.

China's Korean Minority
The Politics of Ethnic Education

Chae-Jin Lee

NEW YORK AND LONDON

First published 1986 by Westview Press

Published 2021 by Routledge
605 Third Avenue, New York, NY 10017
2 Park Square, Milton Park, Abingdon, Oxon OX14 4RN

Routledge is an imprint of the Taylor & Francis Group, an informa business

Copyright © 1986 by Chae-Jin Lee

All rights reserved. No part of this book may be reprinted or reproduced or utilised in any form or by any electronic, mechanical, or other means, now known or hereafter invented, including photocopying and recording, or in any information storage or retrieval system, without permission in writing from the publishers.

Notice:
Product or corporate names may be trademarks or registered trademarks, and are used only for identification and explanation without intent to infringe.

Library of Congress Catalog Card Number: 85-31482

ISBN 13: 978-0-3670-0577-1 (hbk)
ISBN 13: 978-0-3671-5564-3 (pbk)

Contents

	List of Tables	ix
	List of Photographs	x
	Acknowledgments	xi
1.	INTRODUCTION	1
	Notes	13
2.	HISTORICAL SURVEY	15
	Korean Presence in China	15
	Korean Educational Development	30
	Notes	45
3.	THE SEARCH FOR ETHNIC EDUCATION	51
	From the Civil War to the Korean War	51
	Political Autonomy and Ethnic Education	66
	Notes	74
4.	THE PROCESSES OF ETHNIC INTEGRATION	77
	Rectification Movement	77
	Cultural Revolution	88
	Notes	96

5. CURRENT EDUCATION POLICY 99

Ethnic Education Under Four-Modernizations 99
Primary and Secondary Education 114
Higher Education 124
Notes 138

6. ASSESSMENTS AND CONCLUSION 141

Notes 166

Tables

1.1	National Census Data: Minority Nationalities, 1964-1982	3
1.2	Population in Yanbian, 1982	5
1.3	National Census Data: Educational Levels, 1982	7
1.4	National Census Data: Illiteracy and Semi-literacy, 1982	8
2.1	Korean Population in Manchuria, 1881-1943	20
2.2	Korean Population in Yanbian, 1910-1931	34
2.3	Korean Students in Manchuria, 1928	36
2.4	Private Schools Run by Koreans in Yanbian, 1932	39
2.5	Schools Established by Japan in Yanbian, 1932	40
3.1	Population Changes in Yanbian, 1944-1982	53
3.2	Education in Yanbian, 1944-1984	60
5.1	China's Educational Systems, 1981	101
5.2	China's Minority Education and Publications, 1952-1981	102
5.3	Curriculum for Korean Students in Yanbian	121
5.4	Colleges in Yanbian, 1980	125
6.1	Economic Conditions in Yanbian, 1981	157

Photographs

(Photo section follows p. 76)

1. Premier Zhou Enlai (middle) Visiting Yanbian with Chu Tok-hae (right) and Choe Su-han (left) in 1962
2. Yanji Railway Station--Sign Written in Korean, Chinese, and English
3. A Korean Village with Thatched-Roof Houses (1985)
4. Dancers at the Yanbian School of Fine Arts
5. Student Parade in Celebration of the 30th Anniversary of the Yanbian Korean Autonomous Prefecture (1982)
6. A Model Korean Teacher--Kim Chuk-hwa--in Liaoning Province (1982)
7. First Tumen Middle School--Principal Li Pyong-hak and His Daughter (1984)
8. In Front of the New Library of Yanbian University--(from left to right) President Pak Mun-il, Professor Li Hwi-il, Author, Vice-President Chong Pan-ryong, and Professor Choe Yun-gap (1984)

Acknowledgments

During my eight trips to the People's Republic of China since January 1976, I have made a persistent attempt to understand the circumstances of the Korean minority nationality in China. I visited the Yanbian Korean Autonomous Prefecture of Jilin Province (in 1984 and 1985) and other Korean communities, bought a substantial amount of relevant publications, and talked to several hundred Koreans in all walks of life. I was greatly impressed by their uniformly warm hospitality and enthusiastic cooperation. A number of Korean scholars and scientists at Yanbian University, Beijing University, Nankai University, the Central Nationalities Institute, the Chinese Academy of Social Sciences, and the Chinese Academy of Sciences were particularly helpful. They all exhibited a sense of pride in their remarkable educational and cultural accomplishments as a minority nationality. They shared their thoughts and experiences with me and sometimes invited me to their homes and offices. I also held xii

discussions with Han Chinese officials and scholars who are knowledgeable about the Korean minority nationality. In the process I learned much about the historical development of educational programs for China's Korean minority. Even though all of their names are not listed here, I remain extremely grateful to each one of them. For this reason my study is dedicated to the two exemplary leaders of China's Korean minority--Mun Chong-il (former Vice Minister of the State Nationalities Affairs Commission) and Pak Mun-il (Yanbian University President).

I relied upon the Library of Congress and the Hoover Institution Library for major archival materials. The Center for East Asian Studies at the University of Kansas supported and facilitated my research. I am deeply indebted to Professors Chong-Sik Lee (University of Pennsylvania) and Dae-Sook Suh (University of Hawaii), who kindly read part of my manuscript and gave me valuable comments and suggestions. I wish to thank Dr. Key P. Yang (Library of Congress), Vice President Zong Qun (Central Nationalities Institute in Beijing), Professor Kanno Hiroomi (Tokyo University of Foreign Studies), Professors Philip West and Paul Draghi (Indiana University), Dr.Cho Sung-ok (Secretary-General of the Korean National Commission for UNESCO), President Park Il-jae (Korea Research Foundation), Professor Sung Chul Yang (University of Kentucky at Fort Knox), and Dr. Deok Kyo Lee (Oak Ridge National Laboratory) for their encouragement and support. I also gratefully acknowledge the assistance provided by Pam LeRow and

Phyllis McEldowney at the University of Kansas. Of course, I am solely responsible for all contents of this study; hence none of the above-mentioned persons should be held accountable for any aspects of my work.

The romanization of Korean names used in the main text is primarily based on the pronunciation or romanization used by the Korean minority in China; the only exceptions are Syngman Rhee and the Korean residents in the United States. The romanization of Chinese names follows the pinyin system except for Yuan Shih-kai, Chang Tso-lin, Chiang Kai-shek, and other commonly used historical names.

Chae-Jin Lee
Lawrence, Kansas

1
Introduction

According to the Constitution adopted in 1982, the People's Republic of China (PRC) is defined as a "unitary multi-national state" (<u>tongyide duominzu guojia</u>) jointly built by the people of all its nationalities (<u>minzu</u>).[1] Professor Fei Xiaotong (Hsiao-tung Fei), Deputy Director of the Institute of Nationality Studies and a doyen of contemporary Chinese ethnologists, offers a distinction between the Chinese term "<u>minzu</u>" or "nationality" and the European concept of "nation" (also translated as "<u>minzu</u>"); while the former broadly applies to ethnic groups in various stages of development, the latter refers to the rise of nation-states in Western Europe.[2] He suggests that China's long history can be thought of as a complicated pattern of "growth and decline, settlement and migration, integration and disintegration" among a multiplicity of nationalities. Viewed in this historical perspective of ethnic conflict and fusion, the late Fan Wenlan, former Director of the Institute

1

of Modern Chinese History, concluded that the Han nationality, the majority ethnic group in China, is undoubtedly a "mixture of many nationalities."[3]

The 1982 national census shows that the Han population had 936,703,824 (93.3 percent of the total population), while China's 55 officially recognized minority nationalities (shaoshu minzu) were 67,233,254 (6.7 percent of the population). The 15 largest minority nationalities whose populations exceeded one million each were Zhuang, Hui, Uyger, Yi, Miao, Manchu, Tibetan, Mongolian, Tujia, Bouyei, Korean, Dong, Yao, Bai, and Hani (see Table 1.1). In discussing the relationship between the Han and other nationalities, Chairman Mao Zedong once told the Political Bureau of the Chinese Communist Party (CCP)[4]:

> We say China is a country vast in territory, rich in resources and large in population; as a matter of fact, it is the Han nationality whose population is large and the minority nationalities whose territory is vast and whose resources are rich, or at least in all probability their resources under the soil are rich....We must sincerely and actively help the minority nationalities to develop their economy and culture.

Among China's 55 minority nationalities, it is widely believed that the Koreans have the highest level of educational attainment and sustain a strong sense of ethnic identity in their intellectual and cultural activities. They are also considered highly intelligent, hard-working, politically active, and

TABLE 1.1

National Census Data: Minority Nationalities, 1964-1982[a]

| | 1964 | | 1982 | | Increase (1964-82) |
	Numbers	%[b]	Numbers	%[b]	%
China	691,220,104	100.00	1,003,937,078	100.00	45.24
Han	651,296,368	94.22	936,703,824	93.30	43.82
All Minorities	39,923,736	5.75	67,233,254	6.67	68.40
Zhuang	8,386,140	1.21	13,378,162	1.33	59.53
Hui	4,473,147	0.65	7,219,352	0.72	61.39
Uygur	3,996,311	0.58	5,957,112	0.59	49.07
Yi	3,380,960	0.49	5,453,448	0.54	61.30
Miao	2,782,088	0.40	5,030,897	0.50	80.83
Manchu	2,695,675	0.39	4,299,159	0.43	59.48
Tibetan	2,501,174	0.36	3,870,068	0.39	54.73
Mongolian	1,965,766	0.28	3,411,657	0.34	73.55
Tujia	524,755	0.08	2,832,743	0.28	439.82
Bouyei	1,348,055	0.20	2,120,469	0.21	57.30
Korean	1,339,569	0.19	1,763,870	0.18	31.67
Dong	836,123	0.12	1,425,100	0.14	70.44
Yao	857,265	0.12	1,402,676	0.14	63.62
Bai	706,623	0.10	1,131,124	0.11	60.07
Hani	628,727	0.09	1,058,836	0.11	68.41
Kazak	491,637	0.07	907,482	0.09	84.60
Dai	535,389	0.08	839,797	0.08	56.86
Li	438,813	0.06	817,562	0.08	86.31
Lisu	270,628	0.04	480,960	0.05	77.72
She	234,167	0.03	368,832	0.04	57.51

[a]The twenty largest minority nationalities are included in this table.

[b]Percentage of total population in China.

artistically talented. This belief is borne out in the Yanbian Korean Autonomous Prefecture of Jilin Province, which has developed a successful model for minority educational system. A front-page article in China's Renmin Ribao [People's Daily] reported that "the Korean people in Yanbian have a laudable tradition of emphasizing education" and praised their exceptional educational achievements as a stimulus for China's four-modernizations campaign.[5] It also noted the well-balanced four-tier system for formal education in Yanbian: kindergarten, primary school, regular middle and professional schools, and five colleges.

In July 1982 there were about 1.8 million Koreans (chosonjok in Korean or chaoxianzu in Chinese) in China, constituting the 11th largest minority in the country. An overwhelming majority of them resided in the northeastern (Manchurian) region--63 percent in Jilin Province, 25 percent in Heilongjiang Province, and 11 percent in Liaoning Province. About 755,000 Koreans lived in Yanbian alone, with heavy concentration along the Tumen River, but they were only about 40.3 percent of Yanbian's total population (see Table 1.2). Yanbian is approximately the size of Denmark or one-fifth as large as the Korean Peninsula; it has 2 municipalities--Yanji (prefectural capital) and Tumen--and 6 counties--Longjing (formerly Yanji), Helong, Hunchun, Wangqing, Antu, and Dunhua. Dunhua County joined Yanbian in October 1958. Yanbian shares common borders with North Korea (523 kilometers) and the Soviet Union (223 kilometers). The national census also corroborated the popular belief concerning

TABLE 1.2

Population in Yanbian, 1982

	Size(km^2)	Population	Koreans(%)
Yanji City	170	175,957	56.9
Tumen City	530	93,197	58.9
Longjing County	4,210	314,672	65.1
Helong County	4,930	241,600	60.3
Hunchun County	5,290	146,672	56.6
Wangqing County	8,560	264,475	34.0
Antu County	7,510	185,901	28.1
Dunhua County	11,500	449,030	5.3
Total	42,670	1,871,504	40.3

Source: Yonbyon chosonjok jachiju kaehwang [The General Situation of the Yanbian Korean Autonomous Prefecture] (1984).

education among Koreans. Tables 1.3 and 1.4 demonstrate a substantially higher level of educational attainment among the Koreans than among China's total population or other minority nationalities[6].

References to the Korean educational experience are common in Chinese publications. As early as November 1951, Minister of Education Ma Xunlun singled out the Koreans as an outstanding model for minority education.[7] A recent article in Beijing Review stated that "development of education varies from nationality to nationality. For instance, middle schools are quite common in the Yanbian Korean Autonomous Prefecture in Jilin Province while some minorities in more remote regions have not yet popularized primary school education."[8] It also pointed out a rapid increase in the number of Korean minority schools in Liaoning Province; the number of primary schools grew from 175 in 1976 to 271 in 1982, and the number of middle schools grew from 13 to 30 during the same period.[9] "Except for the Mongolians and the Koreans," said another report in Beijing Review, "the percentage of [college] students of other minority nationalities is still below the national average."[10] Moreover, in 1982, an author in Xibei Renkou [Northwestern Population] cited the Yanbian Korean Autonomous Prefecture as the most advanced area in minority educational and cultural life and then identified the Dongs, the Manchus, and the Mongolians as other educationally developed minority nationalities[11]. Recognition of the Koreans' educational and cultural achievements and contributions is not just confined to

TABLE 1.3

National Census Data: Educational Levels, 1982[a]

	College Graduates	College[b] Students	Senior[c] Middle School Students	Junior[c] Middle School Students	Primary[c] School Students
China	72.9	26.4	1,096.6	2,939.2	5,864.7
All Minorities	31.6	11.8	534.8	1,429.5	3,552.7
Korean	175.3	72.5	2,067.5	3,358.8	3,181.3

[a]Numbers per 10,000 persons aged 6 and above.

[b]Includes those who studied but did not finish and those now attending colleges.

[c]Includes graduates, those who attended but did not finish, and those presently enrolled.

TABLE 1.4

National Census Data: Illiteracy and Semi-literacy, 1982[a]

	Male %	Female %	Total %
China	19.17	45.27	31.90
Han	18.48	44.56	31.19
All Minorities	29.71	55.97	42.63
Zhuang	15.73	46.97	31.36
Hui	29.73	53.01	41.22
Uygur	38.70	45.76	42.12
Yi	45.68	77.64	61.56
Miao	39.48	77.48	58.02
Manchu	11.78	23.27	17.03
Tibetan	61.39	87.22	74.83
Mongolian	21.09	36.65	28.55
Tujia	19.93	48.19	33.41
Bouyei	33.78	77.76	55.79
Korean	4.67	15.99	10.45
Dong	25.45	65.64	44.56
Yao	31.55	64.77	47.73
Bai	20.35	60.70	40.76
Hani	56.25	84.15	70.05
Kazak	16.76	27.88	22.14
Dai	45.07	69.12	57.19
Li	27.40	55.65	41.49
Lisu	58.55	85.09	71.92
She	35.17	70.37	51.47

[a]Percentage of illiterates and semi-literates among those aged 12 and above.

Yanbian and other parts of China's northeastern region. A recent reference book, Zhongguo shaoshuminzu [Minority Nationalities in China], stated[12]: "A generation of advanced Korean intellectual elements has grown up. They include several hundred persons working in central state organizations and an additional several hundred members of the research institutes which belong to the Chinese Academy of Sciences in Beijing or the Ministries and Commissions. There are many Korean teachers at colleges and institutes in Beijing and other places in China." In fact, I have personally met with a number of Korean college professors, physicians, writers, poets, artists, journalists, research scientists, and other professional cadres all over China from Beijing and Tianjin to Shenyang and Yanbian.

The Korean example of educational development is conspicuously mentioned for three main reasons: (1) to support and encourage the Koreans' conscious search for cultural and social improvement, (2) to demonstrate a positive and tangible consequence of China's "enlightened" minority policy, and (3) to present a concrete empirical model to be studied and perhaps emulated by China's other minority nationalities. On the 30th anniversary of the founding of the Yanbian Korean Autonomous Prefecture (September 1982), Mun Chong-il (Wen Zhengyi), a Korean Vice Minister of the State Nationalities Affairs Commission and former Chief Administrator of the Yanbian Special District in the late 1940s, specifically stated that other nationalities in China were praising and watching

Yanbian's "distinct development" in the educational, cultural, and scientific fields.[13] A Korean-language magazine, <u>Yonbyon Kyoyuk</u> [Yanbian Education], routinely attributed Yanbian's educational achievements to the wise leadership exercised by the Chinese Communist Party and the State.[14] This official explanation is understandable in the Chinese context, but does not adequately explain why the Korean educational experience contrasts so sharply with the majority of China's other minority nationalities. When discussing the Korean case in July 1981, Zong Qun, a Harvard-educated Vice President of the Central Nationalities Institute, said that the Koreans in China had a "comparatively good economic basis" for educational development.[15] He added that they had benefited from Japanese colonial rule in Manchuria during the 1930s and early 1940s.

Asked about this in October 1983, a senior Yanbian University professor in his mid-60s did not hesitate a minute to quote a traditional Korean saying that parents must educate their children even if they have to sell their precious land or ox. A month earlier, a Korean-American journalist visited a Korean people's commune near Shenyang in Liaoning Province and casually asked an 8-year old girl what she wanted to do when she grew up. She replied in Korean, "I want to go to college."[16] When I had an opportunity to visit a Korean production team with 12 households in the suburb of Tianjin in July 1981, I asked a Korean team leader in his late 40s whether or not he had any particular problems. He said that since his village was far from other Korean communities, his principal problems were to teach Korean to his children and to find appropriate Korean spouses for them.[17] However, he said that the children in his production team attained a higher level of formal education than those in other teams. And in August 1984 when I paid a 5-day visit to Yanbian, I met an ambitious Korean teenager, who anxiously said that his entire future depended upon the results of the national college entrance examinations he had just taken. These four episodes from three different locations (Yanbian, Shenyang, and Tianjin) have a common trait--China's Korean minority, irrespective of location and age, is preserving its traditional cultural heritage which attaches a high priority to the value of education. Education is viewed both as a process of intrinsic cultivation and as the best insurance of survival and upward social mobility in an uncertain environment. It is also a family affair because all members of a Korean family are involved in the educational process. Unlike the Hui, Manchu, and She who all use the Chinese language, the Koreans are vigorously attempting to preserve their own language through their educational programs. It is interesting to note that the Koreans in other countries--the Soviet Union, the United States, and Japan--have an equally strong emphasis on education, but exhibit varying degrees of ethnic self-identity.

The 36-year record of the Korean minority's educational experience in the People's Republic of China (PRC) indicates a complex relationship between their Korean identity and China's shifting minority policy. In general, the Koreans have made a determined, though sometimes tortuous, effort to pursue their own ethnically-based educational goals amidst the subtle, but at times forceful pressure for integration or assimilation into the dominant Han Chinese culture. This effort has been further complicated by a combination of other factors--such as the historical circumstances of Korean immigration to China, the specific characteristics of Korean communities, changing Han-Korean relationships, and, above all, China's fluctuating domestic politics. It is, however, debatable whether, as Professor Wolfram Eberhard suggests, the Han leadership espouses a long-range policy to realize "total integration" of all minority nationalities in China.[18]

Hence this study is designed to explore a set of inter-related questions: Why do Koreans pay so much attention to their own educational programs, especially ethnically-oriented ones? How do they manage the challenges and opportunities of ethnic education within the context of China's political dynamics? What problems and difficulties do they encounter in their search for educational excellence? And how effective is the Korean model for ethnic education in China? These questions will be examined with special focus on the Yanbian Korean Autonomous Prefecture, which has remained a cultural, psychological, and political center for Koreans in China. It is a basic assumption of my study that the issue of educational and cultural autonomy is a vital aspect of China's minority policy.

NOTES

1. See the text of the Constitution, in Beijing Review (December 27, 1982), 10-29, or Renmin Ribao [People's Daily], December 5, 1982.

2. Hsiao-tung Fei, "Ethnic Identification in China," Social Sciences in China, Volume 1, Number 1 (March 1979), 94-107.

3. Fan Wenlan, "Problems of Conflict and Fusion of Nationalities in Chinese History," ibid., 71-93.

4. "On the Ten Major Relationships" (April 25, 1956), in Selected Works of Mao Tse-tung, Volume 5 (Peking: Foreign Languages Press, 1977), 284-307.

5. Renmin Ribao, August 27, 1983.

6. See Zhongguo yijiubaernian renkou pucha baifenzhi she chouyangziliao [Ten Percent Sampling Tabulation of the 1982 Population Census of China] (Beijing: Zhongguo tongji chubanshe, 1983). The only minority nationality that showed a lower rate of illiteracy and semi-literacy were Tartans (8.97 percent), but their total population size (4,127) was negligible.

7. See Ma's report in Minzu zhengce wenxian huipian [Collected Materials on Nationality Policy] (Beijing: Renmin chubanshe, 1953), 69-74.

8. Beijing Review (December 14, 1981), 29-30.

9. Beijing Review (November 29, 1982), 6-7.

10. Beijing Review (October 17, 1983), 16-18.

11. Xibei Renkou [Northwestern Population], Number 2 (1982), 21-27.

12. Zhongguo shaoshuminzu [Minority Nationalities in China] (Beijing: Renmin chubanshe, 1981), 54.

13. The Korean-language text of his speech appeared in Yonbyon Ilbo [Yanbian Daily], September 3, 1982; also see, Renmin Ribao, September 5, 1982.

14. "Minjok chongchaek ul kwanchol hayo minjok kyoyuk ul palchon sikyotta" [We Have Developed Ethnic Education by Realizing Ethnic Policy], in Yonbyon Kyoyuk [Yanbian Education], Number 3 (1979), 6.

15. Interview with Zong Qun, July 13, 1981, Beijing.

16. As reported in the Chicago edition of Hanguk Ilbo, September 12, 1983.

17. On July 12, 1981, I visited a 55-member Korean production team in the Baoyuancun Production Brigade, Xinlicun People's Commune. Pak Chun-bo, a team leader, was a member of the Tianjin Municipal People's Congress.

18. Wolfram Eberhard, China's Minorities: Yesterday and Today (Belmont: Wadsworth Publishing Co., 1982), 103.

2
Historical Survey

Korean Presence in China

Compared with other minority nationalities in China, the history of the Korean minority is a relatively recent phenomenon. Although the Koguryo Dynasty's territories embraced the southern parts of Jilin and Liaoning Provinces between the fourth and seventh centuries, the Yalu and Tumen Rivers served as a natural border between China and Korea for many centuries. The historical record indicates that Korean immigrants lived in China's northeastern region during the 17th and 18th centuries, but in limited numbers. They were mostly seasonal or even illegal migrants because the Manchu leaders of the Qing Dynasty considered the Northeast, especially the Yanbian area, their sacred ancestral homeland and strictly forbade Han and other non-Manchu peoples from disturbing the region. The Choson Dynasty, too, punished those Koreans who surreptitiously entered Manchuria for food, vegetables, and timber.

It was only in 1881 that the Qing government opened the Northeast to settlement by outsiders, mainly to counter the ascendancy of influence of Czarist Russia and Japan, and to aid the migration of poverty-stricken Chinese farmers from Shandong Province. Poor Korean farmers, who suffered from a series of severe famines in Hamgyong Provinces during the 1880s, crossed the narrow Tumen River to China's southern Yanbian area and cultivated land along the River. Likewise, Koreans in Pyongan Provinces crossed the Yalu River to settle in the southern part of Manchuria. In 1881, there were no more than 10,000 Koreans in Yanbian. The lands they cultivated were restricted; in 1885 they measured 50 miles wide and 700 miles long.[1] Manchurian aristocrats and Chinese landowners employed Korean tenant farmers, who built irrigation systems and expanded rice paddies. Four main factors caused the number of Koreans to increase rapidly to 100,000 in Yanbian around the turn of the century: (1) the Qing government's declining authority following the Boxer Rebellion, (2) Russian penetration into Manchuria, (3) Japan's naked colonial ambitions in Korea and Manchuria, and (4) Korea's economic hardships. The growing Korean communities in Manchuria set up their own local self-governing structures (hyangyak). In 1903 the government of the Choson Dynasty dispatched a high-ranking official--Li Pom-yun--to help Korean settlers in what he apparently called "Kando" in Korean for the first time (Jiandao in Chinese and Kanto in Japanese). He organized a private military force to protect the Koreans' life and property.

After the Russo-Japanese War in 1905, Japan established a protectorate over the weakening Choson Dynasty and used the presence of Koreans in Yanbian as one of several excuses for its aggressive penetration into Manchuria. The Japanese supported some Korean residents who argued that Yanbian (or Northern Kando), which the Koguryo Dynasty had ruled, belonged to Korea. In 1907, Ito Hirobumi, the Japanese regent-general in Korea, sent Japanese police constabulary from Hoeryong to Yanji City and pressured the Qing government into accepting Japan's protection of Koreans in Yanbian.[2] At that time there were about 50,000 Korean households in the Yanji area alone and they outnumbered the Han Chinese population by a 4-to-1 ratio. Arguing that Yanbian was an extension of Korean territory, the Japanese opened a Branch Office of the Regency General (Ito's ruling agency in Seoul) headed by Lieutenant Colonel Saito Suejiro in Yanji. In response, the Qing government sent an able military leader, Wu Luzhen (who had studied at the Japanese Military Academy), to Yanji to negotiate a settlement with Col. Saito. After long negotiations, in September 1909 Japan and China signed the Sino-Japanese Agreement on the Tumen River Border between Manchuria and Korea. While Japan recognized the Tumen River as a border between Manchuria and Korea and Yanbian as part of China's sovereign territories, it extracted a number of important concessions from China. China agreed to open Longjing, Yanji, Helong, and Wangqing as trade posts and to accept a Japanese Consulate General in Longjing with branch offices in other cities. Japan also gained the right to repair the Ji-Hui railroad which connected Jilin City to Hoeryong in Korea's North Hamgyong Province. The Japanese also agreed to withdraw their forces from Yanbian within two months. The Chinese government recognized the "residence of Korean subjects" in the demarcated districts of agricultural lands lying north of the Tumen River. Article 4 of the agreement stipulated[3]:

> The Korean subjects residing on agricultural lands within the mixed residence district to the north of the River Tumen shall submit to the laws of China, and shall be amenable to the jurisdiction of the Chinese local officials. Such Korean subjects shall be accorded by the Chinese authorities equal treatment with Chinese subjects, and similarly, in the matter of taxation and all other administrative measures, they shall be placed on equal footing with Chinese subjects. All cases, whether civil or criminal, relating to such Korean subjects shall be heard and decided by the Chinese authorities in accordance with the laws of China, and in a just and equitable manner.

Although all legal cases concerning such Koreans were decided by the local Chinese court, the Japanese Consulate General was permitted to send its representative to attend the court proceedings. Moreover, it stated: "Whenever the Japanese consular officers find that a decision has been given in disregard of law, they shall have right to apply to the

Chinese authorities for a new trial to be conducted by officials specially selected in order to assure justice of the decision." In accordance with Article 5, Koreans were given the right to own land and dwellings, to freely cross the Tumen River in either direction, and to export their products from Yanbian. Meanwhile, by 1910, there were more than a quarter of a million Koreans in Manchuria (Table 2.1); about 95 percent of them came from Hamkyong and Pyongan Provinces. After Japan defeated the Righteous Armies (uibyong) led by Confucian scholars and local yangban in Korea, the patriotic remnants took refuge in Manchuria and Siberia.

As soon as Japan annexed Korea in 1910, it claimed that all Koreans in China were, by definition, Japanese subjects. The Japanese used Koreans as a convenient vehicle for expanding their influence in Manchuria at a time when China was preoccupied with the confusing dynamics of governmental changes and warlord politics. In order to prevent Japan's suspected use of Korean residents in Manchuria, the Chinese government encouraged them to become naturalized Chinese citizens. For this purpose Li Tong-chun, who was Yuan Shih-kai's interpreter in Seoul, became a Chinese citizen himself in Yanbian and founded a pro-Chinese organization (Kanminhoe) in 1909 so that other Koreans could be encouraged to follow his example. The campaign was successful in places like Helong County where almost all Koreans became naturalized Chinese citizens.[4] They thought that this was the best way to protect themselves. This, however, was opposed by a number of

TABLE 2.1

Korean Population in Manchuria, 1881-1943

Years	Numbers	Years	Numbers	
1881[a]	10,000	1924[c]	531,857	
1894[b]	65,000	1925[c]	513,973	
1904[b]	78,000	1926[c]	542,185	
1908[b]	323,808	1927[c]	558,280	
1912[c]	238,403	1928[c]	577,052	(490,000)[b]
1913[c]	252,118	1929[c]	597,677	
1914[c]	271,388	1930[c]	607,119	
1915[c]	282,070	1931[d]	630,982	(595,158)[b]
1916[c]	328,318	1932[d]	672,649	
1917[c]	337,461	1933[d]	673,794	
1918[c]	361,772	1934[d]	719,988	
1919[c]	431,198	1937[b]	968,484	
1920[c]	459,427	1938[b]	1,056,120	(941,903)[e]
1921[c]	488,656	1940[b]	1,145,028	(1,164,483)[e]
1922[c]	515,865	1941[b]	1,300,000	(1,420,564)[e]
1923[c]	528,027	1943[b]	1,414,144	(1,420,564)[e]

[a]Yanbian chaoxianzu zizhizhou gaikuang [The General Situation of the Yanbian Korean Autonomous Prefecture] (1982).

[b]Pak Tu-bok, Zhonggong canjia hanzhan yuanin zhi yanjiu [A Study of the Causes of Communist China's Participation in the Korean War] (1975).

[c]Relations of Japan with Manchuria and Mongolia (1932).

[d]Chong-Sik Lee, The Korean Workers' Party (1979).

[e]Renmin Zhoubao [People's Weekly] (Number 11 in 1950).

conservative Korean leaders (such as Chong An-rip), particularly the Righteous Armies remnants, who set up a counter-organization (Nongmugye) to emphasize an independent Korean identity. Although both organizations shared the common goal of fighting against Japan's rapidly growing presence in Korea and Manchuria, they were unable to reconcile their different methods. Once Yuan Shih-kai solidified his central power in 1913, he ordered the rival Korean organizations disbanded.

The Twenty-One Demands (1915) were another attempt the Japanese made to control China. After Japan and China signed the "Treaty Respecting South Manchuria and Eastern Inner Mongolia" in May 1915 as part of the Twenty-One Demands, the Japanese government insisted that all provisions of this treaty be applied to Koreans in Jiandao. In particular, they invoked Article 3, which stated[5]: "The subjects of Japan shall have liberty to enter, travel and reside in South Manchuria and to carry on business of various kinds-- commercial, industrial and otherwise." Article 2 stipulated: "The subjects of Japan shall be permitted in South Manchuria to lease land necessary either for erecting buildings for various commercial and industrial uses or for agricultural purposes." However, the Chinese government argued that the 1909 agreement, not the 1915 treaty, be applied to Koreans in Jiandao. The Chinese argument was based on Article 8 of the Treaty which stated that "Except as otherwise provided in this Treaty, all existing treaties between Japan and China with respect to Manchuria shall remain in force." The 1915 Treaty was indeed silent on the 1909 agreement.

Notwithstanding the facade of legal disputes, the Koreans in China were caught as the unfortunate, though not always innocent, pawns in a larger political contest between China and Japan. The number of Korean residents in China grew to about 459,000 in 1920 and to about 607,000 in 1930. A large majority of Koreans went to China to avoid economic hardship at home and to seek new opportunities on the bustling Manchurian frontier. According to a survey conducted in the 1920s, 93.6 percent of Korean immigrants in Manchuria cited economic reasons for their exodus from Korea.[6] Others were recruited by Japanese government agencies and industrial organizations in China. Still others escaped Japan's repressive colonial rule in Korea and joined the rising anti-Japanese movements in Manchuria. The New People's Association (Sinminhoe), an anti-Japanese organization in Korea, arranged for Korean nationalists to move to Manchuria so that they could build up a base for Korea's independence movement.

Life for ordinary Korean residents in Manchuria was extremely difficult and precarious in part because the Chinese authorities, plagued by internal disarray and external interference, were unable to preserve law and order during the 1910s and 1920s. The Chang Tso-lin regime at Fengtian (Shenyang) took an ambivalent attitude toward Korean communities. While it was sympathetic toward Korean nationalists, it was under intense Japanese pressure to arrest them in the Sino-Korean border areas as it did in 1920. Many Koreans suffered from a combination of hardship and tragedy--capricious local taxation and economic exploitation, armed banditry, mass atrocities, and various physical punishments. A number of Korean military units were established in Manchuria to conduct small-scale attacks against the Japanese army and police and their Korean collaborators, and to carry armed resistence across the Tumen and Yalu Rivers into Korea proper. This resulted in a mixture of failure and success (such as the effective Qingshanli battle in Helong County in 1920). The Hunchun Incident of 1920 was a notorious example of the Japanese army's atrocities committed against Koreans in Manchuria; in response to a Korean armed attack against the Japanese consular office at Hunchun, Japanese soldiers massacred an entire Korean village.[7] By the end of the 1920s there emerged two broad tendencies in the anti-Japanese Korean resistance groups--Nationalists and Communists.[8] However, neither side had any centralized coordination or leadership.

Disillusioned by the intolerable situation in Manchuria, some Korean immigrants returned home. The ratio of Korean repatriates from Manchuria reached 35 percent between 1917 and 1928.[9] Stories of the Koreans' plight and struggle were numerous; some have been retold in poetry, novels, and movies. For example, the film, "Across the Tumen River," produced by Ra Un-gyu in 1928, described the life and death of a former member of the Righteous Armies in Manchuria. Kim Tong-in's popular essay, "Red Mountain," which he wrote in 1932 following his year-long journey to Korean communities throughout Manchuria, graphically depicted the tragic aspects of Korean farmers exploited by Chinese landlords and the farmers' yearning for Korean independence. One of Korea's best-known contemporary poets, Yun Tong-ju, was born in a Myongdong village of Yanbian in 1917, and studied at the Unjin Primary School and Kwangmyong Middle School in Longjing. Before his death in a Fukuoka prison, he composed the poem, "Counting the Stars," in which he called out, "Mother, You're far off in North Kando [Yanbian]."[10]

The Japanese sponsored and financed a variety of Korean associations in Manchuria--such as the Korean People's Council (Choson inminhoe), the People's Protection Society (Pominhoe), and the Koreans' Association (Chosoninhoe).[11] The Korean People's Council, a form of local self-government, was first organized at Longjing in 1911 under Japanese auspices and quickly spread to other urban Korean communities in Yanbian. By 1928, a substantial proportion of urban Korean households joined it, perhaps under Japanese coercion--76 percent in Longjing, 94 percent in Yanji, and 91 percent in Hunchun. The People's Protection Society was born at Xingjing in 1920 under the former leaders of the Progressive Society (Ilchinhoe), a pro-Japanese political group in Korea. It was an armed self-defense network in those areas where Japanese influence was not strong. Started in 1913, the Koreans' Association based in Andong (now Dandong) was particularly active along the Yalu River. Korean leaders of these and other pro-Japanese local organizations were subjected to assassination and harassment by Korean nationalists and Communists.

In order to control the Korean communities, the governments of Japan and China concluded a secret agreement in 1925; it was signed by Mitsuya Miyamatsu (Chief of the Police Bureau of the Japanese Government-General in Seoul) and Gan Zhen (Chief of the Police Bureau in Fengtian Province).[12] According to the Mitsuya Agreement, Japan and China would cooperate to watch, arrest, and extradite any suspected Korean "recalcitrants," especially those with weapons, in Manchuria. In his Revolutionary Struggle in Manchuria, Professor Chong-Sik Lee states that Koreans in Manchuria suffered heavily as a result of the Mitsuya Agreement. He concludes[13]:

> In many cases, the order to suppress "recalcitrant" or anti-Japanese Koreans became a license for local officials to abuse their authority. Under the pretext of suppressing radicals, Chinese officials and even residents sometimes molested or arrested innocent farmers, extracted large sums of money in "fines," drove them off their land, or killed them. Such outrages, increasingly frequent after 1927, naturally drove many Koreans to desperation, and many of them turned toward the Communist movement.

As Ishii Itaro, a former Japanese Consul-General in Jilin City (from 1929 to 1932), recalls, some Chinese looked down on Koreans with contempt and called them "gaoli fangzi" (Koryo pangja in Korean) in a pejorative sense.[14] At times the Chinese authorities took harsh measures against the Koreans, who were often viewed as agents of Japanese imperialist policy. One unfortunate case of Han-Korean conflict was the Wanbaoshan Incident which took place in 1931 near Changchun[15]. It was indicative of the complicated relationship--both conflict and cooperation--between Koreans and Chinese in Manchuria. The Japanese adroitly instigated or manipulated this relationship to enhance their own interest in Manchuria (and in Korea); Ishii, who had handled this incident, called it a prelude to the "Manchurian Incident," which occured in September 1931.

The establishment of the Manchukuo under Emperor Pu Yi in 1932 changed the legal status of Koreans in China.[16] For all practical purposes Manchukuo was a puppet regime under Japan's firm grip. Japan advanced the notion of harmony among five ethnic groups-- Japanese, Manchus, Mongolians, Koreans, and Han Chinese, but the ethnic stratification was clearly evident. The Koreans in the Manchukuo were permitted to have dual citizenship--Japanese and Manchukuoan. The dual citizenship recognized that although both Han Chinese and Koreans were under Japanese colonial rule in Manchuria, Koreans in general enjoyed a higher legal status than their Han Chinese counterparts. Some Koreans openly supported Japan's policy relative to the Manchurian Incident by giving favorable testimony before the Lytton Commission of the League of Nations. Quite a few Koreans held high government positions in the Manchukuo--Jiandao Provincial Governor (Li Pom-ik and Yun Tae-dong), Lieutenant Governor (Liu Hong-sun), and Consul-General to Poland (Pak Sok-yun).[17] The

Manchurian Army had at least 1,000 Koreans, including those who later became important military leaders in South Korea--Chong Il-kwon (Army Chief of Staff and Prime Minister), Li Han-lim (Superintendent of the Military Academy and Commander of the First Army), Li Ju-il (Army General and Chairman of the Board of Audit and Inspection), Kim Il-hwan (Lieutenant General, Vice Minister of National Defense, and Minister of Home Affairs), and Won Yong-dok (Provost Marshal). Another future South Korean leader, Pak Chong-hi (Deputy Commander of the Second Army and President), graduated from the Manchurian Military Academy and served in the Kwantung Army until 1945. When the conditions of life worsened, however, the Japanese were not reluctant to mistreat Koreans and Chinese; Li Ung, who returned to Seoul in 1979 after a 52-year residence in China, indignantly recalls that while Japanese in Manchuria enjoyed a distinct privilege in ration systems during the Pacific War, they discriminated against Koreans.[18] Another former resident of Manchuria remembers a three-tier rations system in Manchuria. The Japanese easily received rice and a generous supply of sugar, but the Koreans obtained millet and little sugar. However, the Chinese received only sorghum.

In the early 1930s, the Japanese government adopted a 15-year plan to transfer 300,000 Korean rural households (1.5 million people) to Manchukuo for two main reasons--(1) to secure Korean manpower for its imperialist ambitions in Manchuria and Mongolia and (2) to take over farmland in Korea.[19] In 1936 the Manchurian-Korean Development Company was established to organize Koreans' "collective immigration" (<u>chiptan imin</u>) to Manchuria and to provide subsidies and other incentives to the new immigrants. The Manchukuo played an increasingly important part in Japan's strategy, industry, commerce, and logistics, especially after the beginning of the Sino-Japanese War in 1937. Even though the 15-year plan was not fully implemented, the number of Koreans in China passed the million mark in 1938 and reached about 1.3 million in 1941--the year when the Pacific War started. Unlike earlier Korean immigrants, the new ones came from the southern provinces of Korea and moved not only to Yanbian, but also to the northern areas of Manchuria. Since they settled as a group from the same Korean region, they kept their distinct regional characteristics, notably their dialect. With arrangements made by the Manchurian-Korean Development Company, they migrated under the joint auspices of the the Japanese Government-General (Seoul) and the Kwantung Army.

Faced with the Kwantung Army's relentless military pressure, most of the Korean nationalist armed units evacuated Manchuria in the early 1930s. They regrouped in China proper under the leadership of the Korean Provisional Government (led by Kim Ku), which was supported by the Kuomintang (KMT). The Korean Communists in China were also in a state of confusion, but many were admitted to the Chinese Communist Party (CCP). Several thousand young Koreans joined the Northeast Anti-Japanese United Army (NEAJUA) (<u>Dongbei kangri lianjun</u>) organized by the CCP in 1935.[20] Initially there were 11 Armies organized as guerrilla units spread throughout Manchuria. They were reorganized into the First, Second, and Third Route Armies, commanded by Chinese Generals Yang Jingyu, Zhou Baozhong, and Zhao Shangzhi, respectively.

A majority in the Second Army commanded by Wang Detai (Chinese) were Korean recruits from Yanbian and about half of the First and Seventh Armies were also Koreans.[21] The most outstanding Korean leaders of the NEAJUA were Li Hong-gwang (1910-1935), who commanded the First Division of the First Army under Yang Jingyu; Ho Hyong-sik (1909-1942), who commanded the Third Army in 1939 and served as the Chief of Staff for the Third Route Army; and Choe Sok-chon (Choe Yong-gon), who replaced Li Baoman as Commander of the Seventh Army.[22] Later, Choe became the Minister of National Defense and President of North Korea. Other Korean members of the NEAJUA who subsequently assumed top positions in Pyongyang included Kim Il-song (President), Choe Hyon (Minister of National Defense), Kim Chaek (First Vice Premier), Kim Il (Premier and Vice President), Kang Kon (Army Chief of Staff), Kim Kwang-hyop (Minister of National Defense and Vice Premier), and So Chol (Ambassador to China and Vice President).[23] However, in the early 1940s the NEAJUA lost much of its military effectiveness as its leaders--both Chinese and Korean-- retreated to North Manchuria or the Maritime Province of Siberia. Some Korean members moved to the Taihangshan area in North China to join the CCP-sponsored North China Korean Volunteer Army under the leadership of Mu Chong, who participated in the Long March.[24] Mu Chong was closely associated with Kim Tubong, Kim Won-bong, Kim Chang-man, Choe Chang-ik, Pak Il-u, Ho Chong-suk, and Li Sang-jo; after 1945 they all returned to North Korea to obtain high military or administrative positions. A number of Mu Chong's lieutenants in the Korean Voluntary Army--notably, Chu Tok-hae (Zhu Dehai) and Mun Chong-il (Wen Zhengyi)-- rose to important political positions in the People's Republic of China.

Korean Educational Development

The history of Korean educational experiences in Manchuria was heavily influenced by the fluctuating triangular relationship between China, Japan, and Korea and by the changing status of Korean immigrants. As their compatriots did in Siberia and Hawaii, one of the first steps the early Korean residents in China collectively undertook, despite uncertain status and turbulent conditions, was to set up a traditional Korean form of private school (sodang) for their children's education in an alien land. Education was the primary issue discussed by local Korean organizations. Wherever Koreans settled, a proliferation of small Korean schools and, to a lesser extent, Korean churches emerged. New Korean immigrants preferred to move to those places which offered decent educational opportunities for their children. Professor Tsurushima Setsure concludes[25]:

Koreans have traditionally placed great emphasis on education, and Koreans living in Yenpien are no exception. Even at the beginning of the century when Koreans were much poorer than the Han people in the area,

Koreans had more schools. More schools were founded in Yenpien as a result of the "patriotic cultural enlightenment movement," a movement that reached its peak after 1905 and tried to stimulate Korean nationalism by concentrating on culture and enlightenment....It was because of this traditional background that the Korean population was generally better educated than the Han.

The best-known early Korean school in Yanbian was called the Sojon School (sojon sosuk) which Li Sang-sol (a former high official of the Choson Dynasty) and his associates (Li Tong-nyong, Pak Chong-so, and Ryu Jun) established at Longjing in 1906. The school was named after the local area called sojon. It had about 70 students at both the primary and secondary levels; thanks to Li Sang-sol's generous financial contributions, education was offered free of charge.[26] It had a strong anti-Japanese and patriotic curriculum in the Korean language. The curriculum also included modern subjects--such as Mathematics, Geography, the Constitution, and International Law. About the same time Li Tong-chun, a naturalized Chinese citizen, opened a school (Yangjongsuk) in Helong County which emphasized modern education and Chinese language study. In 1907 Li Sang-sol attended the Second International Peace Conference at the Hague as one of the three emissaries dispatched by Emperor Kojong of the Choson Dynasty, and launched a vehement public relations campaign against Japan's aggressive policy in Korea.

In response the angry Japanese authorities forced the Sojon School to close its doors immediately, but its educational mission survived in other places--such as Myongdong School (headed by Pak Chong-so), Waryong Middle School, and Soyongja Middle School. The nationalistic schools attracted as teachers the Confucian remnants of the Righteous Armies as well as progressive Korean intellectuals. The Korean graduates of these schools scattered to other parts of Yanbian to organize numerous primary schools and to spearhead a nationalist and anti-Japanese cultural campaign. After Japan's annexation of Korea, Li Tong-hwi, a returned student from Japan, who immigrated to Yanbian to champion Christianity, assembled anti-Japanese intellectuals, and established a number of Korean primary and middle schools in Longjing, Yanji, and Helong. He commissioned Korean scholars to edit textbooks for Korean students; the books on Korean history and geography were used throughout Yanbian until 1920. Other Korean Christians (such as Kim Yak-yon) and Western missionaries ran several famous schools in Yanbian--Myongdong, Unjin, and Haesong Schools to name a few. The sprawling Christian educational institutions competed with those sponsored by indigenous Korean religious organizations-- Taejonggyo (Tangungyo), Chondogyo, Buddhism, and Confucianism. They included Taesong, Chongil, and Tonghong Schools. Most Korean educators, regardless of their intellectual background, political sentiments, and religious affiliation, shared a common desire to give a good Korean education to their children so that they could resist Japan's imperialist ambitions and restore Korea's independence. The number of schools grew in proportion to the increase of Korean immigrants in Yanbian (Table 2.2). Other areas of Manchuria, too, saw a rapid growth of Korean schools. Professor Pak Yong-sok chronicles the pioneering educational efforts made by two former leaders of the Righteous Armies in Manchuria--Li Sang-yong in Fengtian Province and Li Hwi-yong and his son (Li Kyu-dong) in Jilin Province during the early 1910s.[27] After graduating from the Sinhong School, a Korean military academy in Manchuria, Li Kyu-dong operated a series of Korean schools on his farms. Led by Li Si-yong (future Vice President in South Korea), Li Pom-sok (future Prime Minister in South Korea), Li Tong-nyong, and Li Chong-chon, the Sinhong School produced a large number of Korean military leaders. One of its most celebrated graduates was Yang Lim (Yang Lin), who taught at the Whampoa Military Academy, studied in the Soviet Union, organized anti-Japanese guerrilla activities in Yanbian, and served as a military aide to Mao Zedong during the Long March.[28] A Korean revolutionary--Kim San (or Chang Chi-rak), whose life story Nym Wales (Mrs. Helen Foster Snow) recorded in Song of Ariran-- had attended the Sinhong School.[29]

However, as Japanese power and influence increased in Manchuria during the 1910s and 1920s, the Japanese paid a great deal of attention to Korean educational issues. As soon as the Japanese Regency-General opened its Branch Office in Longjing, it constructed schools for Korean students in 1908, but its offer of generous

TABLE 2.2

Korean Population in Yanbian, 1910-1931

	Koreans	Index	Chinese	Index
1910	109,500	100	33,500	100
1912	163,000	148	49,000	146
1916	203,426	185	60,896	181
1921	307,806	281	73,748	220
1926	356,016	335	86,347	257
1931	396,847	363	120,394	359

Source: Reprinted from The Korean Worker's Party: A Short History (1978) by Chong-Sik Lee with permission of the publisher, Hoover Institution Press.

scholarships and dormitory facilities failed to attract many Korean students in the beginning. They then gave a substantial subsidy to the Kwangmyonghoe (Komeikai in Japanese) headed by a local Japanese leader (Hidaka Heishiro) in Longjing to start religiously oriented schools for Korean students--Yongsin and Kwangmyong Schools.[30] He maintained close ties with the Japanese rulers in Seoul, including Governor-General Saito Makoto. The most outstanding Korean graduate of the Kwangmyong Middle School in Longjing is Chong Il-kwon (future Prime Minister of South Korea); ironically, Longjing also educated Li Chong-ok (future Premier and Vice President of North Korea). The Japanese Government-General in Seoul, Japanese consular offices in Manchuria, and the South Manchuria Railway Company all had direct roles in establishing or subsidizing Korean schools. At the same time the Japanese attempted to influence, suppress, or close anti-Japanese schools in Manchuria; for this purpose they often exerted pressure upon the Chinese authorities by invoking the Mitsuya Agreement.

According to the statistics available, in 1928 more than 29,264 Korean students attended 621 diverse schools in Manchuria.[31] Table 2.3 identifies seven categories of schools classified by Japan: 7 "common" (primary) schools administered by the South Manchuria Railway Company in Fengtian, Harbin, Andong, Tieling, Anshan, Wushun, and Yingkou; 5 schools in Yanbian directly administered by the Japanese Government-General in Seoul and subsidized by the North Hamkgong Provincial government; 54 schools subsidized by the

TABLE 2.3

Korean Students in Manchuria, 1928

	Number of Schools	Number of Students	Number of Teachers
Common schools administered by the South Manchurian Railway Company	7	1,798	49
Schools directly administered by the Japanese Government-General in Seoul	5	2,312	46
Schools subsidized by the Japanese Government-General in Seoul	54	4,123	154
Parochial schools run by religious organizations	108	6,432	259
Private schools run by anti-Japanese organizations	34	?	?
Private schools run by pure Korean organizations	246	7,070	373
Schools established by the Chinese authorities	167	7,529	379

Source: Shimada Michihiro, Manshu kyoikushi [A History of Education in Manchuria].

Japanese Government-General in Seoul via Japanese consular offices and run by Japanese individuals (such as Hitaka), Korean individuals, or pro-Japanese Korean organizations like the Korean People's Council and the Koreans' Association; 108 parochial schools with religious affiliations; 34 private schools run by anti-Japanese Korean nationalist groups; 246 private schools run by politically neutral or pro-Japanese Korean groups; and 167 Chinese schools which accepted both Chinese and Korean students. In addition, there were a small number of Korean students who attended Japanese schools.

In an attempt to rationalize Japan's interference in Korean educational programs and subsequently the Manchurian Incident itself, the Japanese Ministry of Foreign Affairs reported that "zeal for the education of their children becoming more and more intense among the Koreans, they earnestly and unceasingly petitioned the Japanese authorities to establish schools for them"; moreover, Japanese teachers and textbooks were made available to Korean schools.[32] It said that in 1930 Manchuria had "311 schools of all sizes, attended by 21,645 Korean children." Japanese penetration into Korean schools evidently alarmed the Chinese government, which instructed its local authorities (led by Chang Hsueh-liang) to "destroy the common schools and similar educational organs for Koreans under the control of the Japanese government, as these schools teach Japanese and assist towards the realization of Japanese designs on Manchuria and Mongolia."[33] The Chinese authorities sometimes pressed Koreans to adopt

Chinese citizenship, to send their children to Chinese schools, and to hire Chinese teachers in Korean schools. Education for Korean children was a persistent bone of Sino-Japanese contention in Manchuria. Neither Japan nor China was genuinely concerned with the value or integrity of Korean schools. Ishii remembers that the issue of Korean schools was one of his major difficulties in Jilin City in the late 1920s and early 1930s.[34]

This Sino-Japanese competition over Korean schools disappeared in Manchukuo because it was a virtual Japanese puppet regime. In Yanbian 5,388 Korean students attended Korean-run schools; the schools were sponsored by various religious and other organizations (see Table 2.4). Other Korean students attended 16 foreign missionary schools (3,527 students), 38 schools established by Japan (5,719 students) (Table 2.5), and 6 pro-Japanese private schools supported by Japan (873 students). There were also several thousand students in those Korean schools which the Manchukuo government either established or administered in Yanbian. All Korean schools in Manchuria were forced to adopt curriculum and textbooks determined by the Japanese Government-General in Seoul. In this sense Japan regarded the Korean issue in Manchuria as an extension of the Korean Peninsula. The slogans such as naisen ittai [Japan-Korea Unity] and kokoku shinmin no chikai [A Pledge of the Japanese Emperor's Subjects] were invoked to emphasize a sense of spiritual solidarity and common destiny between Japanese and Koreans in

TABLE 2.4

Private Schools Run by Koreans in Yanbian, 1932

	Christian Schools		Korean Religious Schools		Other Schools		Total Schools		Number of Teachers
	Number	Students	Number	Students	Number	Students	Number	Students	
Yanji County	25	1,372	10	785	73	1,791	108a	4,948	163
Helong county	10	461	-	-	9	437	19	898	40
Wangqing County	1	30	-	-	2	94	3	124	7
Hunchun County	3	140	-	-	4	278	7	418	13
Total	39	2,001	10	785	88	2,600	137	5,386	223

Source: Shimada Michihiro, _Manshu kyoikushi_ [A History of Education in Manchuria].

a63 out of 108 schools were not in session.

TABLE 2.5

Schools Established by Japan in Yanbian, 1932

	Number of Schools	Students				Teachers			
		Japanese	Korean	Chinese	Total	Japanese	Korean	Chinese	Total
Yanji County	16	263	3,290	5	3,558	23	56	-	79
Helong County	12	-	1,239	-	1,239	-	35	-	35
Wangqing County	5	20	681	2	703	3	14	-	17
Hunchun County	5	47	509	-	556	5	10	1	16
Total	38[a]	330	5,719	7	6,056	31	115	1	147

Source: Shimada Michihiro, _Manshu kyoikushi_ [A History of Education in Manchuria].

[a] 6 out of 38 schools were not in session.

Korea and Manchuria. Anything related to Korean self-identity was severely restricted.

In 1937 Japan allowed Korean schools to be nominally administered by Manchukuo, but Japanese control of Korean schools was further strengthened during the Pacific War. The Japanese imposed a strict assimilative policy toward Korean residents in Manchuria. As in Korea proper, they forced Koreans to Japanize their names, and attempted to make them second-class citizens of the expanding Japanese Empire. The Han Chinese were classified as third-class citizens. The use of the Korean language was banned in Korean schools, while Japanese was the exclusive medium of instruction. Even Korean songs, dances, and folk festivals were prohibited. A Korean professor at the Chinese Academy of Sciences, who attended a primary school in Longjing City during Japanese rule, remembers that if any student used Korean, all of his classmates received collective punishment. As a result of Japan's fundamentalistic colonial policy in Manchuria, an increasing number of Korean students left the Korean schools and flocked to the Japanese-sponsored ones. The Korean students were encouraged to study technical and vocational subjects rather than liberal arts and were forced to forget their own history.

The Japanese authorities and their Korean collaborators were particularly hostile toward the nationalist schools (exemplified by Taesong and Tonghong Schools), which were a hotbed of Korean nationalist movements and Communist activities. For example, Kim Kon (1903-1937), Pak Chin-u (1908-1935),

Li Il-pyong (1910-1939), and other prominent Korean leaders of the Northeast Anti-Japanese United Army were either teachers or students of the Taesong Middle School in Longjing.[35] A number of nationalist schools were forcibly closed down or significantly weakened, especially immediately before and during the Pacific War. For example, in 1939 the most nationalistic Korean schools in Longjing--Taesong and Tonghong--were merged into one school system under strict Japanese control. And Korean youth were recruited to the Kwantung Army. Under Japanese coercion, missionary schools shut their doors or lost much of their Christian educational mission. A Yanbian University professor, who was a student in a German Catholic school at Longjing, recalls that his school was no different from other Korean schools in only using the Japanese language and showing respect for the Japanese Emperor.

In assessing Japan's educational policy toward Koreans prior to 1945, a Chinese-language book on the Korean minority (published in 1963) angrily commented[36]:

> During Japanese imperialist rule, people's life was extremely poor. The absolute majority of children of workers and peasants were unable to go to school. Even those who entered school with great difficulties received an education of servitude to Japanese imperialism. The Japanese pirates (rikou) practiced an assimilation policy (tonghua zhengce), forced students to study

Japanese language and literature, and strictly prohibited the use of Korean language in educational instruction. They punished those students who used their own language. They promoted the reactionary ideas of feudal morality, poisoned the thoughts of the Korean people, and attempted to paralyze the Korean people's revolutionary consciousness and to nurture loyal servants of the Japanese pirates. All these measures damaged the Koreans' cultural and educational activities.

Another book on China's Korean minority (published in 1982) assails the "Japanese fascist policy which resulted in ignorant masses and ethnic assimilation," which abolished more than 100 private schools run by Koreans in Manchuria, destroyed the Koreans' own history and language, and suppressed progressive and revolutionary teachers and students.[37] However, according to Professor Pak Kyu-chan of Yanbian University (former President), who had graduated from the Tonghong Middle School but had taught at the Kwangmyong Middle School before 1945, Koreans were able to sustain their own private schools in remote rural areas.[38] Even though the goals of colonialism and expansionism dictated Japan's pre-1945 education policy toward Koreans in Manchuria, it is nevertheless undeniable that, as Zong Qun suggested earlier, Japan provided or allowed some educational opportunities for Korean students. In 1944, Yanbian had 557 primary schools (most without advanced classes) with 96,800 students, 18 middle schools (most in vocational training) with 6,700 students, and Longjing Developmental Medical College with 65 students. As a result, Kang Yong-dok (Jiang Yongde), a Korean researcher at the Yanbian Institute on Minority Education, says in his article in Yanbian Daxue Xuebao [Yanbian University Journal] that only 50 percent of Yanbian's Korean children attended primary schools and the rate of illiteracy among Korean adults was more than 80 percent before 1945.[39]

NOTES

1. For a succinct historical background on Koreans in Yanbian, see Yanbian chaoxianzu zizhizhou gaikuang [The General Situation of the Yanbian Korean Autonomous Prefecture] (hereinafter referred to as Yanbian gaikuang) (Yanji: Yanbian lishiyanjiusuo, 1982), 41-48. This important Chinese-language book was published in 1982 to commemorate the 30th anniversary of the founding of the Yanbian Korean Autonomous Prefecture. In 1984 it was republished with some minor revisions both in the Chinese and Korean languages. For the Korean-language version, see Yonhyon chosonjok jachiju kaehwang [The General Situation of the Yanbian Korean Autonomous Prefecture] (Yanji: Yonbyon inmin chulpansa, 1984).

2. For a recent Chinese interpretation of this episode, see Liu Shuguan and Wang Guizhong, "Zhongri yanji bianwu jiaoshe yu Wu Luzhen" [China-Japan Border Negotiations at Yanji and Wu Luzhen], in Zhongri guanxishi luncong [Collected Articles on China-Japan Relations] (Shenyang: Renmin chubanshe, 1982), 194-204.

3. See the agreement in Relations of Japan with Manchuria and Mongolia: Document B (Tokyo: Japanese Ministry of Foreign Affairs, 1932), Appendix, 39-40.

4. Interview with Pak Chang-uk of Yanbian University, August 5, 1984, Yanji.

5. Relations of Japan with Manchuria and Mongolia, 37.

6. Li Hun-gu, Manju wa chosonin [Manchuria and Koreans] (Pyongyang: Sungsil College Publishing House, 1932).

7. See Chong-Sik Lee, The Politics of Korean Nationalism (Berkeley: University of California Press, 1963), 159-164.

8. See Kang Tong-jin, Ilchae ui hanguk chimnyak chongchaeksa [History of Japanese Imperialists' Aggressive Policy in Korea] (Seoul: Hangilsa, 1980), 93.

9. See Lim Chong-guk, Ilchae chimnyak kwa chinilpa [Japanese Imperialist Aggression and Pro-Japanese Collaborators] (Seoul: Chongsa, 1982), 247.

10. See Peter H. Lee, ed., The Silence of Love (Honolulu: University Press of Hawaii, 1980), 78-92.

11. Kang, 253-264, and Lim, 324-359.

12. Kang, 252.

13. Chong-Sik Lee, Revolutionary Struggle in Manchuria: Chinese Communism and Soviet Interest, 1922-1945(Berkeley: University of California Press, 1983), 112.

14. Ishii Itaro, Gaikokan no issho [Life of a Diplomat] (Tokyo: Yomiuri shimbunsha, 1950), 171.

15. For the Wanbaoshan incident, see Chong-Sik Lee,The Politics of Korean Nationalism, 181-183 and 260-261, and Pak Yong-sok, Manbosan sakon yongu [A Study of the Wanbaoshan Incident] (Seoul: Asaea munhwasa, 1978).

16. For a contemporary Chinese assessment of the Manchukuo, see Jiang Niandong and others, Weimanzhouguoshi [A History of the Puppet Manchukuo] (Changchun: Jilin renmin chubanshe, 1980).

17. For a few high-level Korean officials of the Manchukuo, see Tsuboe Senji, Chosen minzoku dokuritsu undo hishi [Secret History of the Korean People's Independence Movement] (Tokyo: Rodo tsushinsha, 1959), 447-449.

18. Interview with Li Ung, August 9, 1983, Seoul.

19. Pak Yong-sok, Hanminjok tongnip undongsa yongu [A Study of the History of the Korean People's Independence Movement] (Seoul: Ilchogak, 1982), 78, and Ko Sung-jae, "Manju nongop imin ui sahoesajok punsok" [A Socio-Historical Analysis of Farmers' Immigration to Manchuria], in Yun Pyong-sok, Sin Yong-ha, and An Pyong-jik, eds., Hanguk kundaesa ron [Studies on Korean Modern History], Volume 1 (Seoul: Chisik munhwasa, 1977), 335-352.

20. For the NEAJUA, see Weimanzhouguoshi, 493-501, and Zhou Erfu, Songhuajiang shangde fengyun [Events along the Sungari River] (Hong Kong: Zhongguo chubanshe, 1947), 29-34.

21. Chaoxianzu jianzhi [A Brief Record of the Korean Nationality] (Changchun: n.p., 1963), 13.

22. For the biography of Li Hong-gwang and Ho Hyong-sik, see Pulmyol ui tusa [Immortal Fighters] (Beijing: Minzu chubanshe, 1982), 9-22 and 107-118, or Pak Mun-il, ed., Ryoksa Sajon [A Dictionary of History] (Yanji: Yanbian renmin chubanshe, 1984), 182 and 589-590.

23. See Dae-Sook Suh, The Korean Communist Movement, 1918-1948 (Princeton: Princeton University Press, 1967), 275, and Chong-Sik Lee, The Korean Workers' Party: A Short History (Stanford: Hoover Institution Press, 1979), 65-66.

24. For the Korean Volunteer Army, see Suh, 220-230, Lee, The Politics, 214-222, and Kim Hak-chol (Jin Xuetie), Hangjon pyolgok [The Song of the Anti-Japanese War] (Mudanjiang: Heilongjiang chaoxianminzu chubanshe, 1983).

25. Setsure Tsurushima, "The Effects of the Cultural Revolution on the Korean Minority in Yenpien," Korean Studies, Volume 3 (1979), 104.

26. Shimada Michihiro, Manshu kyoikushi [A History of Education in Manchuria] (Dalian:Bunkyosha, 1935; reissued by Seishisha, Tokyo, in 1982), 415-417. For a comprehensive biographical study of Li Sang-sol, see Yun Pyong-sok, Li Sang-sol chon [Biography of Li Sang-sol] (Seoul: Ilchogak, 1984).

27. Pak Yong-sok, Hanminjok, 3-51 and 91-133.

28. Pulmyol ui tusa, 1-8.

29. Kim San and Nym Wales, Song of Ariran: The Life Story of a Korean Rebel (New York: John Day Company, 1941). Although Kim told Wales (Edgar Snow's wife) at Yanan in 1937 that he would soon return to the frontline in Manchuria to fight against the Japanese army, he apparently remained at Yanan as an instructor of the Anti-Japanese Military Academy until 1943 when the Chinese Communist Party allegedly executed him on the ground of pro-Japanese espionage activities. Now that the CCP has decided to exonerate him, a group of Korean historians in China is planning to publish a Korean-language edition of this book.

30. Shimada, 418-420.

31. Shimada, 454.

32. Relations of Japan with Manchuria and Mongolia, 75.

33. As quoted in ibid., 76.

34. Ishii, 171.

35. See Pulmyol ui tusa, 217-222, 319-325, and 331-339.

36. Chaoxianzu jianzhi, 112-113.

37. Yanbian gaikuang, 210.

38. Interview with Pak Kyu-chan, August 5, 1984, Yanji.

39. Kang Yong-dok (Jiang Yongde), "Yanbian minzujiaoyu sanshiwuniande lishijingyan" [The 35-Year Historical Experience of Minority Education in Yanbian], in Yanbian Daxue Xuebao [Yanbian University Journal], Numbers 1-2 (1981), 6.

3
The Search for Ethnic Education

<u>From the Civil War to the Korean War</u>

In August 1945, when the Soviet Red Army and a small detachment of the Northeast Anti-Japanese United Force marched into Yanbian, many Koreans were in a state of confusion and dilemma. Some held mass rallies in Longjing and elsewhere to welcome the advancing Soviet soldiers and celebrated the departure of the defeated Japanese. Others began pro-Syngman Rhee activities. Still others decided to return to Korea; this group included those who had collaborated with Japan, those who had been involved in anti-Japanese operations, and those who sought new opportunities in their homeland which was finally liberated from Japan's 35-year colonial yoke. Yet a large majority of the estimated 1.4 million Koreans remained in Manchuria for a variety of reasons--those who had their sources of livelihood in China and therefore decided to stay in China; those who wished to leave, but could not; and those who made no conscious decision, but hesitated to take any action because of inertia or misunderstanding. Members of many families were tragically separated in the confusion. Quite a few Korean peasants were attracted to the CCP's promises to redistribute farmland to tillers and to guarantee ethnic equality (Table 3.1).

In order to fight against the remaining pro-Japanese elements and the pro-Chiang Kai-shek and pro-Syngman Rhee forces in Yanbian, the CCP quickly opened its branch office there in August 1945 and sponsored several organizations for peasants, workers, youth, and women. It also formed a local constabulary to deploy in each county and to keep political and social order. In November the CCP set up a Yanbian Adminstrative Agency to replace the "Jiandao Provisional Government" headed by former Governor Yun Tae-dong. The new Administrative Agency was led by two veteran Han Chinese Communists--Guan Xianting (Chief Administrator) and Dong Kunyi (Deputy Administrator). Other members of the agency were five Han Chinese and six Koreans, including Kang Sin-tae (Kang Kon). Its 10-point policy platform emphasized ethnic equality and ethnic unity and promised to abolish the Japanese colonial educational system.[1] While Han Chinese cadres held the key positions in the Yanbian CCP Committee and the Yanbian Administrative Agency, they cooperated with two groups of Korean Communist military leaders. One group headed by Kang Sin-tae belonged to the Northeast Anti-Japanese United Army under the leadership of Zhou Baozhong. Another group of about 30 cadres led by Mun Chong-il (Wen Zhengyi) belonged to the North China

TABLE 3.1

Population Changes in Yanbian, 1944-1982

	Total Population	Koreans	%Koreans	Han Chinese	%Han Chinese
1944[a]	1,003,352	639,649	63.75	362,916	36.17
1949[a]	835,283	529,262	63.36	288,757	44.57
1952[a]	854,431	529,801	62.01	305,901	35.80
1953[b]	763,763	538,243	70.47	207,560	27.17
1955[c]	774,767	543,800	70.10	213,881	27.60
1959[d]	1,050,800	579,900	55.10	451,900	43.01
1966[a]	1,388,984	646,991	46.58	716,330	51.57
1975[a]	1,683,137	710,901	42.24	941,632	55.95
1979[e]	1,784,098	725,500	40.66	1,027,700	57.60
1980[a]	1,813,791	733,028	40.41	1,048,254	57.79
1982[f]	1,840,982	745,828	40.50	1,060,573	57.60

[a]Kim Sik's Article in Yanbian Daxue Xuebao [Yanbian University Journal] (Number 3 in 1982).

[b]Li Zhenquan, Yanbian chaoxianzu zizhizhou jingji dili [Economic Geography of the Yanbian Korean Autonomous Prefecture] (1957).

[c]Ye Shangzhi and Qun Li, Weida zuguode yanbian chaoxianminzu zizhizhou [The Yanbian Korean Autonomous Prefecture of Our Great Fatherland] (1957).

[d]Chaoxianzu jianzhi [A Brief Record of the Korean Nationality] (1963).

[e]Chon Song-lim's article in Yanbian Daxue Xuebao [Yanbian University Journal] (Numbers 1-2 in 1981).

[f]National Census Data.

Korean Volunteer Army under Mu Chong and moved to the Yanbian Special District via Shenyang in November 1945. The Koreans were assigned to local administrative positions and new military organizations. While Kang commanded a local military unit, Mun served as a Magistrate of Yanji County before becoming a Chief Administrator of the Yanbian Special District. Although there was a sense of rivalry between the two Korean groups, the system of Chinese-Korean ethnic cooperation was thus assured in Yanbian from the beginning.

This was the time when Chairman Mao Zedong recognized the vital importance of defending the liberated areas of Manchuria in the surging CCP-KMT civil war. He issued a directive to the CCP's Northeast Bureau in December 1945[2]:

> Our Party's present task in the Northeast is to build base areas, stable military and political base areas in eastern, northern and western Manchuria. To build such base areas is no easy job; it requires hard and bitter struggle. Three or four years are needed to build such base areas. But a solid preliminary groundwork must be laid in the year 1946. Otherwise we may not be able to stand our ground.

In September 1946 the CCP set up a 27-member Northeast People's Administrative Council chaired by Lin Feng, which included a Korean representative--Kim Kwang-hyop (Jin Guangxia) from Mudanjiang, who later became North Korea's Minister of National Defense and

Vice Premier. He was active in the Northeast Anti-Japanese United Army. The council organized a 4-member Committee on Nationalities Affairs chaired by He A (Mongolian). Other members were Ding Kechuan (Han), Han Yutong (Hui), and Kim Kwang-hyop. Another veteran Korean leader, Chu Tok-hae (Zhu Dehai), was appointed a Director of the Nationalities Affairs Office in Harbin; he had moved from Shenyang to Harbin to lead the Third Branch Unit of the Korean Volunteer Army in late 1945. The council adopted an 8-point platform, in which the CCP promised to eradicate the "fascist servile education" and to implement "democratic people's education."[3] This led to a massive anti-illiteracy campaign in the Northeast. The platform recognized ethnic equality, emphasized ethnic autonomy for Mongolian and Hui peoples, and pledged to respect the languages, cultures, religions, and customs of minority nationalities. It also assured "reasonable protection" for Korean people (hanguoren, not chaoxianzu) and stressed the friendship (yuoyi) between the Chinese and Korean peoples.

Shattered by liberation and civil war, the Japanese-sponsored educational programs for Koreans in Manchuria were suddenly in utter disarray. Many Japanese and Korean teachers departed, all textbooks in Japanese language were abandonded, and some schools were used by the Soviet occupation forces and other government agencies. The governmental educational subsidy was almost non-existent. Hence, just as they had done earlier before Japanese control, Koreans again relied upon their own meager resources and efforts to educate their children amidst fluid and unstable political conditions. The privately-operated Korean schools, which were called minyong hakkyo in Korean or minban xuexiao in Chinese, were established or reestablished all over Manchuria. In Yanbian alone, the numbers of Korean schools and students in the 1946-47 period surpassed those of the pre-1945 era. They also opened a Korean normal school in 1945. A book on Yanbian (1982) vividly describes the extreme difficulty with which Korean parents and teachers set up classrooms and procured chairs, blackboards, pencils, and notebooks for students.[4] Students at all levels started learning Korean script, Hangul, for the first time, studied Korean history and literature, and regarded Korea as their fatherland (choguk or zuguo).

In 1947, Yanbian opened an educational publishing house, which printed about 3.5 million copies of 296 titles and 11 magazines until 1949.[5] However, Yanbian's educational programs were significantly influenced by North Korea, which provided books and teachers. There was no clear concept of a national boundary between Yanbian and North Korea, both of which were under Soviet tutelage. No restrictions were placed on travel across the Tumen River. A Korean historian in China, who lived in Tumen City during 1946 and 1947, remembers that some Korean students crossed the Tumen River to attend their schools on the other side every day and that the residents across the river freely visited their relatives. North Korean scholars frequently visited Yanbian to assist in educational programs. A former Yanbian student remembers that the election campaign for North Korea's Supreme People's Assembly was conducted among Yanbian Koreans in 1948. He also says that when the Democratic People's Republic of Korea (DPRK) was proclaimed in September 1948, all students in his school received from Pyongyang gifts of notebooks decorated with North Korean flags. Mun Chong-il and other Yanbian Korean leaders attended the ceremony for the DPRK's inauguration in Pyongyang and a North Korean leader, Lim Chun-chu, came to Yanbian at Zhou Baozhong's request to serve as a Chief Administrator in 1948. In the meantime, several tens of thousands of Korean youth in China joined first the CCP-controlled Democratic United Force (minzhu lianjun) and then the People's Liberation Army (PLA) under Lin Biao during the Civil War. While Zhongguo shaoshuminzu (1981) mentions that 50,000 Koreans in China served in the PLA during the Civil War, other sources indicate a greater degree of Korean participation.[6] In Yanbian alone 52,000 persons joined the PLA and 85 percent of them were Koreans.[7] In addition, 100,000 persons served in the public security force or militia. On one day (June 4, 1946) 131 boys and girls of the Second Yanji Middle School entered the PLA; this example was followed by students in other schools. About 90 percent of Civil War fatalities from Yanbian (2,917 persons) were Koreans. A Yanbian University professor explained to me that many Koreans fought for the CCP because they were afraid of the KMT's reputed anti-minority policy, and were favorably disposed toward the CCP's promise of ethnic equality and land reform. On the other hand a small detachment of Korean troops led by Kim Hong-il (who later became South Korea's Ambassador to Taipei and Foreign Minister) helped the KMT forces in Shenyang. It was claimed in the Foreign Relations of the United States (1947) that as many as 100,000 Koreans were active in the PLA.[8] Further, the Foreign Relations of the United States (1949) reported that the PLA's 164th and 166th Divisions, consisting of Korean soldiers, moved into North Korea in 1949.[9] They were renamed the 5th and 6th Divisions in the North Korean People's Army; each division had at least 10,000 Korean soldiers.

One of them left a detailed summary of his movement between China and Korea. He was born in Cholla Province in 1927 and moved to Manchuria at the age of 10.[10] He finished his primary education and vocational training in Fengtian Province and became a farmer. In 1946, he joined the PLA and was assigned to the 166th Division in 1948. While he was still in Manchuria, he was admitted to the Korean Workers' Party. In June 1949 his Division moved to Sariwon in Hwanghae Province where it was renamed the 6th Division in the North Korean People's Army. As a platoon commander, he fought in the Korean War and was seriously wounded in Masan near the Pusan perimeter in August 1950. He was cured in a Seoul hospital. In January 1951, he served as a company commander of the 31st Division of the North Korean People's Army in Seoul.

A leading Korean folklorist and author in China-- Chong Kil-un (Zheng Jiyun)--discussed his involvement with the 164th Division and the Korean War in his autobiographical essay.[11] After withdrawing from the Department of Political Economy at Nihon University in Japan, he joined the CCP's New Fourth Army in Jiangsu Province in 1943. He was admitted to the CCP in June 1946. From 1945 to 1949 he served as a political commissar of the 490th Unit of the 164th Division. In August 1949 he joined North Korea's 617th Army as a political officer and took part in the Korean War. He was also an editor of North Korea's "Air Force" magazine. At the end of the Korean War he returned to Yanbian and started his literary and editorial activities. From 1953 to 1974 he had assumed such positions as Vice Chairman of the Yanbian Literary Association, Vice Chairman of the Yanbian Branch of the Chinese Writers' Association, and Editor of the Yanbian People's Publishing House. He wrote and edited several volumes on Korean folk literature.

As the CCP's victory in the Northeast was assured in 1948, the Northeast People's Administrative Council adopted a set of measures to unify educational systems and curricular matters. As Table 3.2 shows, Yanbian had 647 primary schools in 1949, of which 86.7 percent (561 schools) were private schools. Of the 129,000 primary school students, 74.8 percent (94,110) were Koreans.[12] In comparison with the Japanese era, the number of schools increased 16 percent and that of students 34 percent. Yanbian also had 31 middle schools; all but 3 were Korean schools. 22 middle schools were privately administered. There were 13,797 middle school students; 92 percent of them were Koreans. Compared with 1944, the number of middle

TABLE 3.2

Education in Yanbian, 1944-1984

	Primary Schools		Middle Schools	
	Number of Schools	Number of Students	Number of Schools	Number of Students
1944[a]	557	96,800	18	6,700
1949[a]	647	129,800	31	13,797
1957[b]	494	129,860	47	28,890
1960[b]	659	183,488	59	38,776
1979[c]	1,346	274,083	257	209,934
1980[a]	1,300	275,800	241	191,330
1981[d]	1,260	261,200	228	174,100
1984[e]	1,189	NI	226	NI

[a]Yanbian chaoxianzu zizhizhou gaikuang [The General Situation of the Yanbian Korean Autonomous Prefecture] (1982).

[b]Chaoxianzu jianshe [A Brief History of the Korean Nationality] (1964).

[c]Yonbyon Kyoyuk [Yanbian Education] (Number 3 in 1979).

[d]Ibid., Number 9 in 1982.

[e]Ibid., Number 6 in 1984.

schools increased 72 percent and students 89 percent. One of the Korean middle schools was a normal school with 730 students. Yanbian had 4,596 teachers; 76.3 percent of them were Koreans. The spread of Korean schools was evident in other parts of China's northeastern region. For example, in 1949, Heilongjiang Province had 188 Korean primary schools (24,600 students) and 10 Korean middle schools (2,000 students).[13]

It was also in April 1949 that the Northeast Korean People's University (a predecessor to Yanbian University) was established at Yanji under a Korean President--Chu Tok-hae (Zhu Dehai), a new Chief Administrator of the Yanbian Administrative Agency. He argued that higher education was essential to the improvement of Koreans' economic and social conditions in China.[14] He was assisted by Professor Lim Min-ho, who was in charge of the university's day-to-day administration. Staffed by about 60 teachers, it admitted 490 students and offered courses in Arts, Sciences, Medicine, Agronomy, and Engineering. All instruction was given in the Korean language. The Koreans in China are proud of the fact that they opened the first minority institution of higher learning in China six months before the birth of the PRC. At that time there were only two other universities in Jilin Province--Jilin University and Northeast People's Normal College in Changchun. Hence this university has been a symbol for Koreans' ethnically conscious educational programs in China.

The Korean War disrupted Yanbian's educational progress. The "Resist-America and Aid-Korea" campaign was particularly intense among Koreans in China. Students in Yanbian were required to spend three hours a week studying the political dimensions of this campaign, particularly the importance of patriotism and internationalism. They were also mobilized to write letters of support to Chinese and North Korean soldiers and to collect bags of gifts for them. A Korean scientist, who was a student of the Longjing Middle School during the Korean War, recalls that his school was used by North Korean troops and his classroom was overcrowded by North Korean refugee students, particularly the children of high North Korean officials. He says that students were cautioned about America's bacteriological warfare devices. Kim Il-song's oldest son--Kim Jong-il--attended a Chinese school in Jilin City during and immediately after the Korean War. It is reported that 4,600 Yanbian Koreans, including many middle school students, joined the Chinese People's Volunteers (CPV) in Korea. In addition, 3,600 civilians took part in the Korean War for political works, translation and interpretation, and logistical support.[15] Another source states that 8,000 Yanbian youth joined the CPV, another group of 5,740 served as support personnel, and of the 6,981 boys and girls from Yanbian who died in Korea 98 percent were Koreans.[16] Other areas of China sent Koreans to participate in the CPV; for example, 1,330 Koreans from a Hailong County of Liaoning Province went to the war and 486 Koreans from a Hailin County of

Heilongjiang Province did so in December 1950.[17] Many other Korean youths crossed the Tumen and Yalu Rivers and directly joined the North Korean People's Army. About 1,000 Korean nurses served during the war. Mun Chong-il served as a CPV general throughout the war and assumed an important political role in Korea.

A Korean professor of the Central Nationalities Institute remembers that all of his schoolmates (about 500) in Yanbian University enthusiastically volunteered to go to the Korean War, but they were rejected on the ground that they would be needed as minority cadres (minjok ganbu or minzu ganbu) in China. Likewise, in November 1950, 717 students and teachers of the Yanbian Normal School signed a petition to Chairman Mao Zedong in which they asked for the permission to go to the war.[18] 584 students at the Tumen Middle School did the same. Apparently the Koreans in China, especially the students, had a strong sense of solidarity with North Korea at this time. They were particularly aroused by alleged U.S. bombing attacks against a Korean primary school in Helong County, a Korean village in Changbai County, and a railway station in Yanji County, during November 1950. It was also reported that the U.S. air raid killed innocent Koreans along the Yalu River.[19] They lavishly celebrated the CPV's capture of Pyongyang and Seoul. A Korean soldier from Yanbian, who entered the Korean War, published a poem in a Korean-language newspaper (Tongbuk Choson Inminbo published in Yanji) and proclaimed that he was fighting for the protection of his family and property back in Yanbian.[20]

In a moving diary written in Korean and Chinese characters, one of the Yanbian Korean volunteers described his first encounter with his ancestral homeland and his joy in crossing the 38th Parallel.[21] The diary starts on January 13, 1951, and ends on March 20, 1951. He was probably killed or captured as a prisoner of war on that date. On January 28, he says: "I took the first step to Korea, the place of my activities and operations. Distant mountains are full of pine trees, which are as green as if the spring already came. I saw a few old men in white clothes and the orderly display of classic tile-roof houses. I felt the superior quality of the Korean race." On March 6, he writes: "At last I fulfilled my dream today--the dream to cross the 38th Parallel. When I put my feet on the southern side of the Parallel for the first time, I was truly overwhelmed by boiling excitement and determination."

One of the most famous Korean poets in China--Kim Chol (Jin Zhe)--tells his experience of the Korean War in his autobiographical essay.[22] In 1950, at the age of 18, he quit his teaching job at a Korean primary school in Heilongjiang Province and joined the Chinese People's Volunteers in Korea. Inspired by his own war experience, he composed two volumes of poems in Korean. He also wrote and directed a play entitled "The Dance of Army Engineers," which received the highest award at a national contest sponsored by the People's Liberation Army. When this play was shown at Beijing during the Korean War, he had an opportunity to meet with Chairman Mao Zedong. After the war he returned to Yanbian as a journalist for the Northeast Korean People's Daily (Tongbuk Choson Inminbo). He continued to publish his poems, which focused on the history of the Korean people's struggle against Japan in China. Although he was imprisoned during the Cultural Revolution and denounced as a "revisionist," a "reactionary authority," and an "anti-party and anti-socialist element," he subsequently resumed a very productive literary life. The collections of his narrative poems--Tongtul muryop [Dawn] and Saebyol chon [Life of the Morning Star]--are favorably reviewed by Professor Peter H. Lee in Korean Studies.[23] Kim has held a number of important positions--Vice Chairman of the Yanbian Literary Association, Secretary-General of the Yanbian Branch of the Chinese Writers' Association, Vice Chairman of the Jilin Provincial Branch of the Chinese Writers' Association, and Member of the Association's Committee on Minority Literature.

It was, however, in 1950 during the Korean War that the Chinese government transformed Korean private schools into public schools (gongban xuexiao), consolidated the number of Korean schools, and required that all Korean students in the fifth grade and above start learning the Chinese language. Under Premier Zhou Enlai's auspices, the First National Conference on Minority Education was held in Beijing for 9 days in September 1951 with 126 participants, including Korean representatives. The Conference stressed the need to educate minority students in their own languages and to allocate special government funds for this purpose. It also urged that methods for ethnic education be consistent with the stage and level of each nationality's historical development. Making a report on this Conference to the Central People's Government Council in November 1951, Minister of Education Ma Xulun cited the Korean case as an advanced example of minority education.[24] He said that about 92 percent of Korean children studied at primary schools and that 25,870 Korean students attended 57 middle schools. In the Yanbian Special District, he said, there was one middle school student per 35 people, while some minorities in Sichuan and Yunnan Provinces had no formal schools at any level. Likewise, Liu Geping, a Hui Vice Minister of the State Nationalities Affairs Commission, praised the early educational achievements among the Korean minority nationality.[25]

Political Autonomy and Ethnic Education

The new attention paid to the issue of minority education was accompanied by the Regulations on Autonomy of Minority Areas which the State Council adopted on February 22, 1952, and the Central People's Government Council ratified on August 8, 1952. Accordingly, the Yanbian Korean Autonomous Region (qu) was established on September 3, 1952 under the leadership of Chu Tok-hae (Zhu Dehai); after the adoption of the Chinese Constitution, it became the Yanbian Korean Autonomous Prefecture (zhou) in December 1955. The Yanbian People's Government was led by Chu as Chief Administrator and two Deputy Administrators-- Dong Yukun (Han) and Choe Chae (Cui Cai) (Korean). Choe, a literary figure, had served as Chu's lieutenant in the Third Branch Unit of the North China Korean

Volunteer Army at Harbin. The Government had 15 agencies and departments; 11 were headed by Koreans. Among 300 deputies to the Yanbian People's Congress, there were 209 Koreans (69.7 percent), 76 Han Chinese (26.3 percent), one Hui, one Manchu, and one Mongolian. The proportion of the Korean legislative representation was higher than the size of the total Korean population (62 percent) in Yanbian. Moreover, 78 percent of all cadres in Yanbian (7,814) were Koreans. The number of Korean cadres in education was even higher (87 percent). The autonomous status for Korean communities was available in other parts of the Northeast. In Heilongjiang Province there were 5 Korean Autonomous Districts and 101 Korean Autonomous Villages in 1952. They were merged into 33 Korean xiang in 1956. Liaoning Province and Inner Mongolian Autonomous Region had 3 Korean xiang each and Jilin Province had 7 Korean xiang and one Korean-Manchu xiang.[26] One of Jilin's Korean xiang was elevated to the Changbai Korean Autonomous County (xian) in 1958.

The Korean minority's autonomous status provided a clear political and administrative framework for their ethnic education. In 1952 the Yanbian People's Government decided to issue all official documents in both Chinese and Korean languages and set up a government bureau to translate Chinese documents into Korean. Each county government had staff members responsible for translation. Court documents and signs for railroad and bus stations and other public places were written in both languages. However, all publications in Korean script avoided using Chinese characters except for scholarly works. About this time the PRC and North Korea agreed upon the citizenship status of Koreans in China; all Koreans living in China's northeastern region (outside Shanhaiguan Pass) were automatically recognized as Chinese citizens, but other Koreans had a choice between Chinese and North Korean citizenship. Several thousand Koreans opted for the North Korean citizenship. In order to become Chinese citizens, they needed the approval of the governments of China and North Korea.

Yanbian's autonomous structure further encouraged the expansion of educational programs for Koreans in China's northeastern region as a whole. The Second National Conference on Minority Education, held in June 1956, adopted a 12-year plan (1) to strengthen instruction in minority languages, (2) to produce minority-language textbooks, and (3) to train minority teaching staff.[27] This decision was consistent with Chairman Mao Zedong's speech delivered at the CCP Political Bureau two months earlier. Discussing the relationship between the Han and the minority nationalities in China, he pointed out the danger of Han chauvinism more than local-nationality chauvinism.[28] He also criticized the Soviet Union's minority policy.

In Yanbian, primary schools had been almost universally accessible since 1952, when 85 percent of all school-age children and more than 90 percent of Korean children attended primary schools. The Yanbian People's Government earmarked 35 percent of its annual budget for education during the First Five-Year

Economic Plan (1953-1957). Economic resources for education increased significantly during this period. The budget for education in 1958 showed a 94.6 percent increase over the 1952 figure. Hence Kang Yong-dok calls this period (1952-58) a "golden age of minority education" in Yanbian.[29]

After the Korean War Yanbian became an ideologically relaxed center where a Korean cultural and educational renaissance took place. During this golden age it absorbed an influx of Korean intellectuals and educators from other areas of the Northeast. The Koreans felt proud of being Korean and aggressively asserted their ethnic identity as distinct from the Han Chinese civilization. This neo-traditionalist upsurge was reflected in their educational, literary, artistic, and social activities. They emphasized the importance of maintaining single-ethnic schools at all levels--primary, secondary, and higher educational programs. Korean schools were clearly separated from their Han Chinese counterparts. Even in an ethnically mixed school there were separate classes for Korean and Han Chinese students. Use of the Korean language flourished in all Korean schools, including Yanbian University. The Koreans regarded their schools as better than the Han Chinese schools and sometimes felt that they were intellectually and culturally superior to all other ethnic groups in China. The graduates of the First Yanbian Middle School, an elite Korean school, produced 69 percent and 91 percent of those Yanbian students who gained admission to colleges in 1957 and 1958, respectively.

The Korean cultural climate in Yanbian was optimistic and buoyant. Novels, essays, and poems written in Korean contained a unique Korean flavor; they depicted the heroic history of Koreans' anti-Japanese struggles, praised Koreans' independent-minded character and strong ethnic identity, and encouraged the preservation of Korean social values and customs. This trend was especially prevalent during the Hundred Flowers Campaign. The Yanbian Assocation for Literature was organized by Korean writers in 1950 and published a popular Korean-language magazine, Yanbian Munye [Yanbian Literature], in 1953. In 1956 the Yanbian Branch of the Chinese Writers' Association and an Assocation for Korean Folk Literature were established. In order to preserve and spread Korean cultural messages, libraries, museums, theatres, and social clubs were expanded and folk festivals, athletic events, and ethnic customs were greatly promoted. Korean performing arts--traditional dance, music, and drama--were revived. The artistic talents of Choe Mison (dancer) and Chong Yul-song (composer) were nationally acclaimed.[30] Chong, who taught at the Anti-Japanese Military Academy at Yanan, joined the North China Korean Volunteer Army, and took part in the Korean War, composed such popular songs as "The Marching Song of the People's Liberation Army," "The Choir of the Eighth Route Army," "The Marching Song of the Korean Volunteer Army," and "The Marching Song of the Chinese People's Volunteers." Hence Li Zhenquan observed[31]:

The development of culture and education has been even more rapid (than economic development). Yanbian is one of the districts of China which has achieved universal primary school education. It is also one of the minority nationality areas in the nation which has the highest cultural level....Graceful and elegant Korean dancers have brought to light their national tradition of excellent art. They have toured the nation's capital and other places, and their performance was well received. The Korean people as a nationality are experts in singing and dancing, and their spare-time cultural activities are carried out everywhere. The Korean people love athletic activities even more.

In 1955 Korean educators developed a systematic plan for editing textbooks in Korean literature. The plan spelled out two major guidelines--(1) to include a proper mix of works from classical and contemporary contemporary Korean literature, Chinese literature, and foreign literature (primarily, Soviet works) and (2) to inspire in the students a love of their own ethnic literary heritage.[32]

Ye Shangzhi and Qun Li reported that by 1956 Yanbian had 40 secondary (middle) schools--33 junior middle schools (27 Korean schools, 4 Han schools, and 2 Korean-Han mixed schools), 4 senior middle schools (3 Korean schools and 1 Han school), and 3 normal schools--and that there were 26,492 middle school students.[33] According to them, Yanbian University had become a fine comprehensive institution of higher learning with 1,207 students. All but 7 auditors were Koreans. Students used the most advanced scientific equipment manufactured by China, the Soviet Union, and East European nations. Under the presidency of Chu Tok-hae, who stressed the importance of Yanbian University's existence in the frontier region, it was able to obtain a more favorable teacher-student ratio (1 vs. 2.4) than the country's average ratio (1 vs. 3.1).[34] In 1957, Yanbian opened several professional middle schools to train Korean teachers with competence in Korean or Chinese languages and other specialized vocational middle schools in fine arts, public health, and agronomy. By 1958 middle schools were widely available to Korean students in Yanbian and illiteracy was almost wiped out among the youth. In 1958 Yanbian Medical College and Yanbian Agricultural College were separated from Yanbian University. The Yanbian Engineering College opened, too, but it was closed three years later due to lack of funds. In the midst of the Great Leap Forward Movement in May 1958, Yanbian set up a Saebyok (Liming or Ryomyong) Sparetime Farmers' College in Dongcheng People's Commune in Longing under the celebrated leadership of Kim Si-ryong, a "national labor model" and a member of the National People's Congress; as a program to enhance the technological ability of Korean peasants, it was much heralded as the first such school in China.[35]

The enthusiasm for education was pervasive among Koreans in other parts of China. The Changbai Korean Autonomous County in Jilin Province had 60 primary schools with 4,740 students in 1959; the number of students grew 13 percent in 10 years, and it accommodated about 98 percent of school-age children.[36] It also operated 9 secondary schools with 1,000 students--3 regular middle schools and 6 work-study vocational schools. Likewise, Lianoning Province had 24,100 Korean students in primary schools, 6,560 in junior middle schools, and 960 in senior middle schools.[37]

NOTES

1. <u>Yanbian gaikuang</u>, 88-89. The membership of the agency and its platform are displayed in the Yanbian Museum (Yanji).

2. <u>Selected Works of Mao Tse-tung</u>, Volume 4 (Peking; Foreign Languages Press, 1961), 81.

3. Zhou Erfu, 80-83.

4. <u>Yanbian gaikuang</u>, 210.

5. Ye Shangzhi and Qun Li, <u>Weida zuguode yanbian chaoxianminzu zizhizhou</u> [The Yanbian Korean Autonomous Prefecture of Our Great Fatherland] (Beijing: Minzu chubanshe, 1957), 66.

6. <u>Zhongguo shaoshuminzu</u>, 50.

7. <u>Yanbian gaikuang</u>, 112.

8. <u>Foreign Relations of the United States: 1947</u>, Volume 7 (Washington: USGPO, 1972), 249.

9. <u>Foreign Relations of the United States: 1949</u>, Volume 8 (Washington: USGPO, 1978), 574.

10. National Archives, SA-2012, Box-5, File-109.

11. See Wu Chongyang and Tao Lifan, eds., <u>Zhongguo shaoshuminzu xiandai zuojia chuanlue</u> [Biographies of China's Contemporary Minority Authors] (Xining: Qinghai renmin chubanshe, 1982), 241-242.

12. <u>Yanbian gaikuang</u>, 211.

13. <u>Chaoxianzu jianzhi</u>, 113.

14. As quoted in Li Hwi-il (Li Xiyi), "Shenqie huainian laoxiaozhang Zhu Dehai tongzhi" [Deeply Remember Old President--Comrade Chu Tok-hae], <u>Yanbian Daxue Xuebao</u>,Number 3 (1982), 2.

15. <u>Zhongguo shaoshuminzu</u>, 51.

16. Yanbian gaikuang, 122.

17. Tongbuk Choson Inminbo [Northeast Korean People's Daily], December 17, 1950.

18. Yanbian gaikuang, 120-122.

19. For example, see a report in Tongbuk Choson Inminbo, December 16, 1950.

20. Ibid., December 9, 1950.

21. National Archives, SA-2012, Box-7, File-62.

22. Wu and Tao, 217-223.

23. Korean Studies, Volume 5 (1981), 160-164

24. See Ma's report dated November 23, 1951, in Minzu zhengce wenxian huipian, 69-74.

25. See the text of Liu's report dated September 21, 1952, in Minzu zhengce wenjian huipian [Collected Documents on Nationality Policy], Volume 1 (Beijing: Renmin chubanshe, 1958), 92-98.

26. Chaoxianzu jianshi [Brief History of the Korean Nationality] (Changchun: n.p., 1964), 172.

27. Yonbyon Kyoyuk, Number 9 (1982), 7.

28. Selected Works of Mao Tse-tung, Volume 5, 295-296.

29. Kang Yong-dok, 8.

30. For information about Choe Mi-son, see Renmin Ribao, September 12 and 14, 1981, and for Chong Yul-song, see the recollections by his widow--Ding Xuesong (Chinese Ambassador to the Netherlands in 1979-1981) in Renmin Ribao, November 26, 1981.

31. Li Chen-chuan (Li Zhenquan), Yanbian chaoxianzu zizhizhou jingji dili (Shanghai: Xinzhishe chubanshe, 1957), translated as Economic Geography of the Yen-pien Korean Autonomous Chou (New York: U.S. Joint Publications Research Service, 1959), 44.

76

32. As cited in <u>Yonbyon Kyoyuk</u>, Number 9 (1982), 11-13.

33. Ye Shangzhi and Qun Li, 61-62.

34. Li Hwi-il, "Shenqie huainian," 2.

35. This college was officially called <u>Ryomyong upyo nongmin taehak</u> in Korean or <u>Liming yeyu nongmin daxue</u> in Chinese, but Koreans commonly refer to it as <u>Saebyok taehak</u> [Dawn College] because <u>saebyok</u> means dawn in vernacular Korean language; <u>ryomyong</u> also means dawn, but it is borrowed from <u>liming</u> in Chinese.

36. <u>Chaoxianzu jianzhi</u>, 117.

37. Ibid., 117-118.

4
The Processes
of Ethnic Integration

Rectification Movement

While opportunities for ethnically-based education in Yanbian expanded substantially during the 1950s, the radical leftist swing in Chinese politics during the Rectification Movement (1957-1959) negatively affected minority education. Chinese leaders pursued an ideologically-inspired monistic and integrationist policy toward minority nationalities and gave a higher priority to the ultimate goals of national unity and political centralization than to social diversity and ethnic autonomy. As Henry Schwarz notes, there was a "rising tide of mutual recrimination and discrimination" between Han and non-Han nationalities in China.[1]

The Rectification Movement (chongpung undong or zhengfeng yundong) had a two-stage development in Yanbian. The first stage lasted from May 1957 to June 1958, during the aftermath of the Hundred Flowers Campaign when minority intellectuals had openly criticized the symptoms of Han chauvinism. It was mainly directed against anti-party "deviationists" and "capitalistic rightwing elements." In response to the CCP's "Instructions on Rectification" issued in April 1957, the Yanbian leadership conducted a campaign against three erroneous tendencies--"bureaucratism," "splitism" (or "sectarianism"), and "subjectivism" among its cadres. When the CCP's "Instructions on Organizing Forces and Preparing Counterattacks against Rightwing Elements" were issued in June 1957, they held a series of meetings in Yanbian and launched an intensive anti-rightwing movement. In his Inter-Party Directive of June 1957, Chairman Mao Zedong stated[2]:

> Organize forums at colleges and universities to let professors speak their minds about the Party, and as far as possible try to get the Rightists to spew out all their venom, which will be published in the newspapers. Let the professors make speeches and let the students respond freely. Better let the reactionary professors, lecturers, assistants and students spew out their venom and speech without any inhibitions. They are the best teachers....This is a great political and ideological struggle.

For this reason the Yanbian Committee of the CCP sponsored several meetings with professors, intellectuals, artists, and other leaders of culture, industry, and commerce during the summer of 1957. The Jilin Provincial Committee of the CCP convened a session of minority cadres in Yanbian. The Yanbian

People's Congress and the Yanbian Committee of the Chinese People's Political Consultative Conference also organized meetings and rallies to criticize rightwing elements. A recent book on Yanbian (1982) points out that the campaign against capitalistic rightwing elements was "completely necessary" at the time, but that its excessive efforts led to an "unfortunate result" which mistakenly labeled some patriotic persons as rightwing elements.[3]

The second stage coincided with the Great Leap Forward Movement, especially massive irrigation works during the winter of 1957 and people's communes in the summer of 1958· following the model of Dongcheng People's Commune established on August 29, 1958, 925 advanced agricultural cooperatives in Yanbian were organized into 78 people's communes by the end of September 1958. Encouraged by this sweeping radicalism, the anti-rightwing campaign was specifically directed against minority leadership, who were identified as anti-party, anti-socialist, and anti-Han Chinese. It was therefore called a "nationality rectification movement". (minzu zhengfeng yundong). In Yanbian, the second-stage campaign was launched against the "capitalistic rightists" and "local ethnic nationalists" (difang minzu zhuyizhe), who allegedly promoted particularlistic minority interests at the cost of China's national interests. A book on China's Korean minority, which was written in 1958 and 1959, but published in 1964, stated[4]:

> Under the excuse of helping the party's rectification movement, a small number of

capitalistic rightwing elements and local ethnic nationalists are launching an attack against the party and socialism. The rightwing elements in the areas where Korean nationality live, like other rightwing elements all over China, agitate to blow fire everywhere, spread innuendo, attack the party's leadership, oppose the agricultural cooperative movement, oppose the anti-reactionary campaign, and disrupt the party's unified purchasing policy. While wearing the cloak of "protecting minority interests," they attack the party in regard to the problems of minority nationalities. They conspire to split the fatherland, clamor about the "grand autonomy of all Koreans in the northeast," accuse the CCP of being the "party of Han Chinese," and promote the reactionary "theory of ethnic superiority."

Evidently there were some Korean cadres and intellectuals who argued that they were of a superior race than that of the Han Chinese and who complained that Han Chinese monopolized the top party positions in Yanbian despite the facade of ethnic autonomy. They probably advanced the notion of a grand unity of all Koreans in the Northeast; some even implied that Yanbian, part of Koguryo's territories, should belong to Korea. According to Ye and Qun, a small number of Korean nationalist elements argued that "autonomy is

Premier Zhou Enlai (middle) Visiting Yanbian with Chu Tok-hae (right) and Choe Su-han (left) in 1962

Yanji Railway Station--Sign Written in Korean, Chinese, and English

A Korean Village with Thatched-Roof Houses (1985)

Dancers at the Yanbian School of Fine Arts

Student Parade in Celebration of the 30th Anniversary of the Yanbian Korean Autonomous Prefecture (1982)

A Model Korean Teacher--Kim Chuk-hwa-- in Liaoning Province (1982)

First Tumen Middle School--Principal Li Pyong-hak and his Daughter (1984)

In Front of the New Library of Yanbian University-- (from left to right) President Pak Mun-il, Professor Li Hwi-il, Author, Vice President Chong Pan-ryong, and Professor Choe Yun-gap (1984)

bad, but independence is good," thus manifesting their "political ambitions."[5]

The 1964 book declared that the conflict between socialism and minority nationalism was a "long-range, complicated, and sharpened class struggle between proletarian and capitalist consciousness." It warned that the "poisonous influence" was prevalent among Korean capitalists and intellectuals, who advocated the "thesis of multiple fatherlands" (presumably, both China and Korea) and the "purification of minority languages." The Koreans probably articulated that the Korean language be purged of Chinese influence and restored to its pure traditional form. Yet the Chinese government stipulated that "any plea for the preservation of purity of the existing minority languages must be resolutely attacked."[6] The Korean rightwing elements, the 1964 book said, needed "class education" (jieji jiaoyu) to eradicate their ethnically-inspired bourgeois ideas and to inculcate a higher level of patriotism (aiguo zhuyi) and a notion of "united fatherland and ethnic unity" (zuguode tongyi he minzu tuanjie). The book further stated[7]:

> In our big united family of nationalities, Han Chinese are the central nationality (zhuti minzu) because they have a large population, a long history, and relatively rapid development in political, economic, and cultural areas. This is a result of our historical development. In order to repel imperialist aggression, to construct the socialist fatherland, and to promote each

nationality's development and prosperity, it is vitally important for all nationalities to strengthen their unity under the central leadership of Han Chinese.

More specifically, Koreans in China were required to learn from the Han nationality's "advanced culture and experience" and to increase the number of hours devoted to Chinese-language studies. As June Dreyer points out, emphasis on the Chinese language was intended to remove linguistic barriers to national unity.[8] A high priority was attached to the Chinese language as a "common tool" of communications for all nationalities. It was made a primary medium of instruction in ethnic education programs; even first-grade Korean students were required to study the Chinese language. A correspondent of <u>Renmin Ribao</u> reported in 1958 that the cadres of Korean nationality in various government organs initiated a campaign to study the Chinese language in the spring of 1958 and regarded it as a fundamental measure for becoming "Red" and "Expert."[9] He critically asserted that some people of Korean nationality had a vague idea concerning the Han - nationality, erroneously regarded the Han nationality as backward, and considered themselves superior and that they deviated toward linguistic "conservatism and isolationism" by arguing that the pure Korean language should not be invaded by Han terminology. He even mentioned that some Korean nationalistic elements attacked those Korean cadres who spoke in the Chinese language by saying that they were harmful to the dignity of the Korean nationality.

Textbooks in Korean literature were discarded on the grounds that they were spreading local nationalism and confusing Korean students' concept of fatherland and of destroying the unity of ethnic groups. The government revised the textbooks on the basis of "mass-line education," transformed Korean literature classes into political indoctrination sessions, and extensively used newspaper editorials and commentaries. An increasing number of Korean-language textbooks included translations from Chinese-language textbooks; "foreign materials," "foreign words," and "foreign poets" were excised from Korean-language books and magazines.[10] In September 1958 the government convened a national meeting of minority-language publishers in Beijing and criticized any literary manifestation of local nationalism. It issued an unmistakable instruction[11]:

> We must expand Chinese literature in detail, but shorten foreign literary works, reduce the old ones and increase the contemporary ones, adopt the unified nation-wide textbooks as the main ones, and use ethnic textbooks only as supplementary readings. The combination of supplementary ethnic materials, classical ethnic works, and foreign works should not exceed 30 percent in a literary textbook.

The First Congress of the Yanbian CCP held in November 1959 reaffirmed the continuing relevance of anti-rightist rectification campaigns.

84

The government banned a number of indigenous Korean literary works which stressed the uniqueness or superiority of Korean cultural characteristics. Several hundred Korean educators and intellectuals were labeled "rightwing elements" and "local ethnic nationalists" and removed from their positions. A number of Korean schools were merged with Han Chinese schools under the rationale that ethnic discrimination should be uprooted. The idea of ethnically mixed schools (minjok ryonhap hakkyo or minzu lianhe xuexiao) was given preference over single-ethnic schools (tanilhan minjok hakkyo or danyi minzu xuexiao). A symbol of Korean cultural uniqueness, Yanbian University admitted Han Chinese students in 1959, invited Han Chinese to teach, and offered some substantive courses in the Chinese language. A Yanbian University professor recalls that although only a few Korean professors were directly subjected to criticism or harassment, they remained "very nervous" throughout the Rectification Movement. He admits that some Korean intellectuals in Yanbian carelessly advocated the notion of Korean superiority, but he recognizes Chu Tok-hae's crucial role in containing the anti-rightist campaign in Yanbian University.

In retrospect, a recent book on Yanbian maintains that it was necessary to criticize and educate those minority cadres and intellectuals who held erroneous views, but the campaign became an "atrocious struggle" and "inhuman attack."[12] Moreover, Kang Yong-dok points out the leftist mistakes committed in 1958 and 1959 under the pretext of ethnic amalgamation (minzu ronghe). According to him, the leftists "disregarded the importance of minority affairs, forgot about the longevity of minority existence, and mistook nationalities as an empty historical category which would disappear very quickly."[13] Nevertheless, Korean zeal for educational advancement survived. So Tsurushima Setsure observes that "by 1959, Yenpien was known as China's leader in terms of literacy. Education was not only widely diffused but Yenpien students ranked highest academically of all the national minority areas."[14] In fact, the people's commune movement saw a proliferation of locally-administered schools; about 90 new middle schools sprung up, an average of 1.7 schools per commune.[15] About 90 percent of primary school graduates moved on to middle schools in Yanbian. In Yanji City, Helong County and Hunchun County (which had a large concentration of Korean population), it reached 95 percent. Likewise, in 1959 the Changbai Korean Autonomous County had about 1,000 secondary school students who attended 3 regular middle schools and 6 vocational schools.[16] In Liaoning Province, too, a large number of Korean students (6,560) were at various middle schools. Even though this rapid spread of educational opportunities had some positive aspects, the quality of secondary education inevitably suffered in Yanbian. In subsequent years, some Yanbian educators criticized this "vicious" and "blind" expansion under conditions which were not yet suitable.[17]

As the Great Leap Forward Movement and its extreme leftist measures were replaced by a more moderate policy in the early 1960s, the rigid restrictions on Korean minority educational programs were eased somewhat. The chinese government relaxed the notion of ethnic amalgamation. In 1961 Li Weihan (Minister of the State Nationalities Affairs Commission and Director of the CCP Department of United Front Work) declared that the disappearance of ethnic differences may be possible in a Communist society, but not in a socialist one.[18]

However, there was always a time lag in implementing a new central policy in remote corners of China such as Yanbian. Moreover, the Koreans tended to be somewhat authoritarian in their social and political behavior and very cautious in adjusting themselves to the prevailing national mood of ideological relaxation. The Yanbian leaders, still led by Chu Tok-hae, started separating the ethnically mixed schools into Korean and Han Chinese schools by 1962, and organized an editorial board (under Kim Mun-bo, Yanbian CCP Secretary) to revise school textbooks in the Korean and Chinese languages. They attached renewed importance to studies in Korean and exempted the first-grade Korean students from learning Chinese. At Yanbian University, 45 percent of the courses were taught in Chinese during 1962. The Ministry of Education issued a series of new directives in 1962 to stress basic (less ideologically oriented) education in primary and secondary schools and to restore programs for ethnic education.

Accordingly, in November 1963, Kim Mun-bo announced an outline for Korean-language education:[19]

> The Korean language is a basic tool that students must have to study all other subjects. If they study the Korean language well, it helps their understanding of Mathematics, Physics, Chemistry, Biology, History, Geography, and other fields. If not, they will not only face an adverse effect in their studies and intellectual growth, but also have a difficult problem in promoting ethnic culture and socialist construction.

The outline stipulated that textbooks in Korean literature must include more works written by Korean authors and must be consistent with the grammatical rules of the Korean language as well as Korean "language customs."

In the early 1960s, the Chinese leaders in Beijing paid keen personal attention to Yanbian, especially because it occupied a politically sensitive geographic position in China's changing relationship with the Soviet Union and North Korea. On June 22, 1962, Premier Zhou Enlai came to Yanbian University. A Yanbian University professor recalls that the Premier did not follow a guided campus tour, but rather made his own instant decisions to inspect whatever facilities he wanted to see. He paid an unscheduled visit to a student dormitory and its kitchen. He even opened the lid of a rice cooker, examined it, and said, "This is clean." He also toured both the Yanbian

Medical College and the Yanbian Agricultural College. To the delight of Koreans in Yanbian, he managed to express simple greetings in the Korean language.[20] About two years thereafter Zhu De (Chairman of the Standing Committee of the National People's Congress) and Dong Biwu (Vice Chairman of the People's Republic of China) inspected Yanbian University and other educational and cultural facilities in Yanbian. The Korean political and educational leadership were greatly encouraged by such top-level visitors. The moderation of China's minority educational policy was rather short-lived because the CCP conducted a socialist education campaign--another form of rectification movement--in 1963 and then launched the Great Proletarian Cultural Revolution in 1966.

Cultural Revolution

The Cultural Revolution, which threatened the basic premises of China's minority policy altogether, had a devastating impact upon minority education everywhere in China. The impact was particularly severe in Yanbian because the political and ideological struggles among Koreans were extremely ferocious and brutal. The established Korean leadership long headed by Chu Tok-hae was completely deposed; like Ulanhu in Inner Mongolia, Chu was accused of being a representative of "China's Khrushchev" (Liu Shaoqi) and of protecting his "independent kingdom." His earlier studies in the Soviet Union and his visits to North Korea were cited to "prove" that he was a foreign spy; his "treason" was publicly denounced. Furthermore, he was accused of having proposed to the Chinese government that China offer substantial territorial concessions over the Chonji (Heavenly Lake) to Kim Il-song. Directed by Mao Yuanxin (Mao Zedong's nephew and a close associate of Jiang Qing), who moved from the Harbin Military Engineering College with his followers to Yanji in January 1967, a group of young Korean radicals led by Choe Hae-ryong (Cui Hailong, a local militia leader in Hunchun) joined Han Chinese Red Guards in faithfully executing the Cultural Revolution directives in Yanbian. They attacked Yanbian University as a "black bastion of the Chu Tok-hae local nationalism" and physically persecuted Li Hwi-il (Li Xiyi; Yanbian University CCP Secretary) and other professors as stooges of Chu Tok-hae.[21] Anti-Chu wall posters and Red Guard publications were rampant on campus.

A recent book on Yanbian (1982) reveals the gruesome magnitude of human sacrifice during the Cultural Revolution--about 4,000 persons died due to persecution, about 5,000 were wounded, and several tens of thousands were imprisoned, isolated, or investigated.[22] In the midst of factional struggles in Yanbian, some Koreans crossed the Tumen River and fled to North Korea. Moreover, the border areas were politically strained because the Red Guard publications assailed Kim Il-song as a "fat revisionist." Premier Zhou Enlai dispatched Song Rengiong (Alternate Member of the Political Bureau and Political Commissar of the Shenyang Military Region) to Yanbian to save Chu from the rampaging Red Guards in September 1966 and recalled Chu to Beijing for his personal safety in April 1967;

transferred to a Hubei commune in October 1969, he died in July 1972 at the age of 61.[23] (In May 1978 the Jilin Provincial Committee of the Chinese Communist Party decided to restore Chu's honor posthumously.)

At the height of the Cultural Revolution the Shenyang Military Region Command placed Yanbian under martial law; Mao Yuanxin himself became the Region's Political Commissar. As Mao's protege, Choe Hae-ryong took over the Yanbian Revolutionary Committee; he was elected to the 9th CCP Central Committee as an Alternate Member in 1969 and to the 10th CCP Central Committee as a Regular Member in 1973. In 1975 he was a member of the Standing Committee of the National People's Congress and a Political Commissar of the Jilin Military District; after the fall of the "Gang of Four" and Mao Yuanxin, Choe was stripped of all public positions in 1977. He lost the CCP membership as well.

In 1979, the Yanbian Education Bureau reported on the adverse effects of the Cultural Revolution on Korean education in Yanbian as follows[24]:

> For a decade since 1966, our prefecture's minority education received a historically unprecedented calamity due to the destruction by Lin Biao and the Gang of Four. The special characteristics of minority education were annihilated, the use of minority language was discarded and restricted, and the programs to train minority teaching personnel and to produce minority-language textbooks were thoroughly destroyed. Three professional middle schools disappeared and

two senior middle schools were transformed into professional middle schools. Although Yanbian University was fortunately retained, it was so mercilessly trampled upon that it lost the character of a minority institution....The rate of student drop-out increased and the proportion of illiterate and semi-illiterate youth increased to 13.9 percent. The quality of teachers at all levels of schools declined drastically.

The ten-year calamity that befell ethnically-based educational systems in Yanbian and other Korean communities in China was reminiscent. of the Rectification Movement (1957-1959), but the Cultural Revolution exerted a far more fundamental and pervasive impact. Just as in the rectification campaign, the radicals targeted the use of Korean language in primary and secondary schools for assault. Guided by the notions of ethnic assimilation (tonghua) and amalgamation (ronghe), they argued that the Korean language would be utterly useless in a matter of 10 or 15 years and would eventually become a foreign language in China. There was a wide-spread propaganda campaign to promote the idea that the use of ethnic language meant cultural degeneration and political retreat. Influenced by this rhetoric and concerned about the future career interests of their children, an increasing number of Korean parents took their sons and daughters out of Korean schools and sent them to Han Chinese schools. Consequently, the proportion of Korean students in Yanbian who attended Han Chinese

92

schools reached 25 percent in middle schools and 13 percent in primary schools in 1976.[25] They were largely illiterate in the Korean language.

In other areas of Jilin Province, Korean middle schools were closed because the students transferred to Han Chinese schools en masse. Classes for Korean students in an ethnically mixed schools were no more than an appendage. Students remaining in Korean schools were required to spend more time in learning Chinese at the cost of their native tongue. In Yanbian's senior middle schools, Korean language courses were all eliminated and the hours for Korean language classes in primary schools and junior middle schools were reduced by half.[26] Governmental expenditures for Korean schools were appreciably cut. A few professional middle schools switched instruction from Korean to Chinese languages. The Yanbian Normal School was dispersed to each county and thus its educational quality declined dramatically. At Yanbian University, the Department of Korean Language and Literature was subsumed under the Department of Chinese Literature as a specialty. All instruction was given in the Chinese language except for courses in Korean Linguistics and Korean Literary Selections.

Korean poets and writers were also under attack. For example, a noted Korean playwright, Hwang Pong-ryong, was severely persecuted on the ground that his popular play, "The Son of Changbaek" (published in 1959), which dramatized the history of the Koreans' anti-Japanese struggles in the Changbaek (Changbai) Mountain area, glorified the unique contributions made by Korean revolutionaries and thus de-emphasized the important roles played by Han Chinese revolutionaries.[27] Kim Chol, Kim Hak-chol, and many other Korean authors were imprisoned. And Kim Changgol gave up writing novels in the Korean language, and instead devoted himself to translating The Dream of the Red Chamber and other Chinese classics into Korean.

There was a movement to integrate ethnically separate schools; in 1965 more than 90 percent of Yanbian schools were single-ethnic schools. This percentage decreased throughout the Cultural Revolution. The idea of ethnically united or mixed schools (minzu lianhe xuexiao) was advanced on the grounds of eliminating the perpetuation of ethnic differences, but Koreans regarded it as an effective way of sinification and of promoting great Han chauvinism. "In such ethnically mixed schools," the Yanbian Education Bureau pointed out, "students used separate textbooks, separate languages, and separate curricula. This situation prevented the implementation of uniform educational guidance and the conduct of careful political education, and made it difficult to enhance the quality of the teaching staff. A variety of artificial difficulties occurred as a result."[28] The reality was not a full integration of educational programs, but rather an unproductive and uneasy coexistence of ethnically separate programs in an ethnically mixed school.

The Cultural Revolution stopped or restricted publication of Korean-language materials--books, newspapers, magazines, and reference materials.

Textbooks were particularly hard-hit. Korean books in libraries were either destroyed or simply unavailable. Korean-language textbooks were not allowed to include works originally written in the Korean language, but were required to use translations from common national textbooks written in the Chinese language. Hence the new textbooks failed to reflect the Koreans' unique cultural background, social customs, and linguistic characteristics. The quality of Korean-language textbooks declined considerably, and the availability of Korean-language reference materials and extra-curricular readings was limited. It was emphasized that courses in Korean language and literature must serve as a way "to strengthen clear class consciousness and militant socialist culture and to consolidate the dictatorship of the proletariat."[29] The intrinsic value of ethnically-based education was completely abjured. A Korean professor at Beijing University notes that Korean-language books published during the Cultural Revolution relied upon the direct and mechanical translations of Chinese terms and phrases and were therefore incomprehensible to Korean students; the worst example was the Korean-language edition of Selected Works of Chairman Mao Zedong (Volume 4). Yonbyon Ilbo [Yanbian Daily], a Korean-language newspaper, was a mere translation of its Chinese-language edition. And the confusion and delay in preparing textbooks caused an acute problem of textbook shortages in Korean schools.

A large number of Korean teaching staff were dismissed, demoted, persecuted, or investigated. Many were sent to farms and factories for political reeducation and "labor reform". Professors Li Hwi-il and Pak Mun-il and other Yanbian University leaders spent three or more years in the May 7th cadre schools. Because Yanbian Medical College and Yanbian Agricultural College were closed and Yanbian University was only partially open, only 250 teachers remained on the three campuses in 1970--a decline of 76.3 percent from 1966. Reduced to a 3-year program, Yanbian University adopted an "open-door admission" policy to accept soldiers, workers, and farmers not according to their intellectual ability, but rather on the basis of their political commitment and class background. The ratio of Korean students dwindled to less than 30 percent. For all practical purposes Yanbian University lost its Korean character.

NOTES

1. Henry G. Schwarz, "The Treatment of Minorities," in Michel Oksenberg, ed., China's Developmental Experience (New York: Praeger Publishers, 1973), 203.

2. Selected Works of Mao Tse-tung, Volume 5, 449.

3. Yanbian gaikuang, 135.

4. Chaoxianzu jianshi, 209.

5. Ye Shangzhi and Qun Li, 18.

6. As quoted in Henry G. Schwarz, "Communist Language Policies for China's Ethnic Minorities: The First Decade," China Quarterly (October-December 1962), 175.

7. Chaoxianzu jianshi, 212-213.

8. June Teufel Dreyer, China's Forty Millions: Minority Nationalities and National Integration in the People's Republic of China (Cambridge: Harvard University Press, 1976), 160-161.

9. See Renmin Ribao, October 4, 1958. Professor Chong-Sik Lee drew my attention to this important report.

10. Dreyer, 157.

11. As quoted in Yonbyon Kyoyuk, Number 9 (1982), 13.

12. Yanbian gaikuang, 135.

13. Kang Yong-dok, 8.

14. Tsurushima, 104.

15. Yanbian gaikuang, 214.

16. Chaoxianzu jianzhi, 117-118.

17. Yonbyon Kyoyuk, Number 6 (1984), 4-5, or Number 9 (1982), 6-11.

18. See Li's lengthy speech given at a conference of Xinjiang cadres in September 1961 in Li Weihan, Tongyi

zhanxian wenti yu minzu wenti [The Problems of United Front Work and Nationalities] (Beijing: Renmin chubanshe, 1981), 520-581.

19. As quoted in Yonbyon Kyoyuk, Number 10 (1982), 43.

20. As reported in Jilin Ribao, January 8, 1977.

21. Li Hwi-il, "Shenqie huainian," 4.

22. Yanbian gaikuang, 137. This specific statistical information concerning the Cultural Revolution casualties is omitted in Yonbyon chosonjok jachiju kaehwang (1984).

23. For Chu's biographical information, see Donald Klein and Ann B. Clark, Biographical Dictionary of Chinese Communism, 1921-1965 (Cambridge: Harvard University Press, 1971), Volume 1, 254-256, and Pak Mun-il, Ryoksa sajon, 418-419.

24. Yonbyon Kyoyuk, Number 3 (1979), 2.

25. Ibid., 3.

26. Yonbyon Kyoyuk, Number 10 (1982), 40.

27. Wu and Tao, 316-319.

28. Yonbyon Kyoyuk, Number 3 (1979), 4.

29. As quoted in Yonbyon Kyoyuk, Number 10 (1982), 44.

5
Current Education Policy

Ethnic Education under Four-Modernizations

Since the downfall of the "Gang of Four" the Chinese leaders have adopted a pragmatic and conciliatory policy toward minority nationalities for a host of reasons. First of all, they wanted to reduce, if not eliminate, pent-up tensions and conflicts in minority areas and to restore a sense of peace and cooperation among different nationalities, who mostly inhabit sensitive border areas. Second, as they did for many Han Chinese, they attempted to redress the enormous injustices and sacrifices inflicted upon minority cadres and intellectual leaders, who had been particularly subjected to humiliation and harassment during the Cultural Revolution. Third, in keeping with China's new emphasis on four-modernizations, they encouraged minority nationalities to increase their educational and technological levels so that they can develop the rich untapped natural resources of their areas. The mobilization of minority nationalities'

100

positive cooperation was sought on the basis of persuasion, incentive, and reward rather than through coercion, intimidation, and punishment. Fourth, they are convinced that a new policy allowing a greater degree of ethnic identity and local autonomy is compatible with China's long-range national interests. They believe that ethnic assimilation or amalgamation is an unrealistic, impatient, and counter-productive goal, unachievable until a full-fledged Communist society is established. Also, the Han Chinese leaders assured themselves that they can influence, control, and lead minority nationalities. They regained their confidence in exerting control over all minority areas (Tables 5.1 and 5.2).

The Education Bureau in Yanji County stated the main objectives of ethnically oriented educational programs:[1]

The development of ethnic education is needed to uplift China's scientific and cultural standards, to promote unity among all nationalities, to construct frontier areas, and to strengthen national defense. It is also necessary for carrying out the policy of minority autonomy, creating a precondition for training in minority languages, and producing human resources for four-modernizations. In sum, ethnic education has a significant strategic meaning.

Guided by this new orientation toward minority nationalities, the Chinese government restored the use of minority languages, provided additional funds for

TABLE 5.1

China's Educational Systems, 1981

	China				Minority Nationalities		
	Number of Schools	Number of Students	Teaching Staff	Other Staff	Number of Students	Teaching Staff	Other Staff
Higher Education:	704	1,279,500	249,900	416,400	51,200	8,400	11,500
Secondary Education:	112,505	50,145,500	3,008,800	1,108,300	1,862,300	112,400	43,300
Regular Middle Schools	106,718	48,595,600	2,844,000	901,400	1,770,600	105,200	
Specialized Middle Schools	3,132	1,069,000	135,900	189,800	78,100	6,300	8,000
Agricultural and Vocational Middle Schools	2,655	480,900	28,900	17,100	13,600	900	600
Primary Education:	894,074	143,328,300	5,580,100	584,500	7,355,700	330,600	44,700
Kindergartens:	130,296	10,562,000	401,100	197,800	41,700	6,200	2,500

Source: Zhongguo Baike Nianjian [Chinese Yearbook] (1982).

TABLE 5.2

China's Minority Education and Publications, 1952-1981

	1952	1957	1965	1978	1981
Minority Students:					
Higher Education	2,900	16,100	21,900	36,000	51,200
Secondary Education	92,000	314,300	390,700	2,526,000	1,862,300
Primary Education	1,474,200	3,194,300	4,350,000	7,686,000	7,355,700
Minority Teachers:					
Higher Education	623[a]	1,941	3,311	5,876	8,364
Secondary Education	2,700[a]	9,100	16,100	116,900	112,300
Primary Education	59,800[a]	81,100	133,200	310,200	330,600
Circulation of Books in Minority Languages:	6,612,000	14,616,000	24,800,000	39,080,000	26,520,000
Circulation of Magazines in Minority Languages:	1,686,000	2,438,000	2,680,000	3,130,000	5,900,000
Circulation of Newspapers in Minority Languages:	29,333,000	24,335,000	39,550,000	70,720,000	91,950,000

Source: Zhonguo Jingji Nianjian [Chinese Economic Yearbook] (1982) and Beijing Review (May 23, 1983).

[a]indicates as of 1953.

construction of minority schools, developed textbooks in minority languages, and paid more attention to training minority cadres and teachers. In Liaoning Province where Koreans constituted only 0.5% of the total population, for example, the government assigned additional staff members to minority schools at the ratio of 0.7 person per each minority class. It also increased annual educational subsidies to minority students from 3 to 5 yuan per student in primary schools and from 14 to 20 yuan per student in middle schools. Chen Beichen (Han Chinese), Vice Governor of Liaoning Province, refuted as erroneous the notion that ethnic education should not be given high priority at a time when China's overall education is under-financed and when minority nationalities are being assimilated. He maintained that the equality and unity among ethnic groups was essential to China's best national interests.[2] A Liaoning Korean educator declared[3]:

> All nationalities in our country are equal. Each nationality has a right to develop its own ethnic education and our socialist system has an obligation to assure it. It is not a waste of money to support ethnic schools even if the number of ethnic students is small; rather it represents the correctness of the Party's minority policy and the superiority of our socialist system. This is something that we can be proud of in the world. We must confidently nurture ethnic schools and produce good minority human resources.

104

Symbolically, the Fifth National People's Congress printed its ballots in 6 languages--Chinese, Korean, Mongolian, Tibetan, Uygur, and Kazakh.[4] In order to increase the college enrollment of minority students, the Ministry of Education allowed them to take the national college entrance examinations in their own languages, admitted them to college with lower test scores than their Han Chinese peers, and established a minimum quota for minority college students in the autonomous areas.[5] In the Inner Mongolian Autonomous Region, for instance, the minimum quota for Mongolian college freshmen was 25 percent, while the total Mongolian population was only 14 percent of the total in that region. It was an "affirmative action" measure to readjust cases of historical inequality.[6] Furthermore, the Third National Conference on Minority Education, which the Ministry of Education and the State Nationalities Affairs Commission (reactivated in 1978) jointly sponsored in February 1981, agreed to institute 5-year minority student classes (minzuban) in China's 10 key universities (such as Beijing Unibersity, Qinghua University, and Zhongshan University) and 21 other colleges.[7] Admitted with lower than passing scores, several hundred minority students enter the best institutions of higher learning each year. They take one year of specially structured remedial courses and then enter the regular 4-year course work with Han Chinese students.

In Yanbian, the new policy of giving college entrance examinations in minority languages was welcomed as a major boost for Korean language studies in primary and secondary schools. The best Korean students in Yanbian were therefore able to enter Beijing University, Qinghua University, Nankai University, and other premier institutions without going through the minzuban system. The only Korean minzuban was available in the Northeast Normal College at Changchun. The Korean students in Jilin Province were allotted 5 additional points in their college entrance examination scores--the lowest bonus among all minority aspirants. Out of the maximum possible score of 600 points, Jilin Province in 1984 established a cutoff score of 400 points for college admissions. It was one of the highest cutoff points in the country; they were determined by each provincial unit. A Yanbian University professor argued that since Korean students were doing so well in college entrance examinations anyway, they should decline 5 additional points out of national pride. However, another professor noted that even a one-point difference affected about 1,000 students in Jilin Province. Moreover, according to Professor Pak Kyu-chan, those Korean students who took entrance examinations in their native tongue did much better in the field of Language and Literature (about 10 points higher on the average) than their Han competitors because that field (120 total points) was divided into Chinese and Korean sections. Hence President Pak Mun-il of Yanbian University declared that a Korean student cannot say that he failed in the college entrance examinations because he did not know the Chinese language.[8]

A 19-year old female Korean student (Miss Chang), whom I met at one of China's best national universities in July 1981, was a graduate of the First Yanbian Senior Middle School (an elite Korean school) and a freshman specializing in Japanese language in the Department of Foreign Languages. She took her college entrance examinations in Korean. Although her Korean had a thick northern Hamgyong accent, her Japanese pronunciation was excellent. She said that 85 percent of her classmates moved on to colleges and quite a few of them were admitted to nationally prominent colleges. In 1981 her university had 12 Korean minority students, who, together with Korean staff members, maintained close social associations. Another 22-year old Korean female student (Miss Kim) specializing in English literature was unable to speak Korean well; born in Beijing as a daughter of a military officer, she had not had an opportunity to study at a Korean school. Her parents sent her to a people's commune in Yanbian for two years to learn Korean language and social customs. However, unlike Miss Chang, she used Chinese in her college entrance examinations. Her English was very good. In 1983, a Korean professor at Beijing University said that his school had about 40 Korean minority students, mostly in the science departments. As minority students in a non-ethnic school, both Miss Chang and Miss Kim received an additional government allowance (2 yuan per month) on top of their regular stipends. In ethnic schools such as Yanbian University, Korean students received 100 percent of their educational subsidy (17.5 yuan a month), while an average of only 85 percent was given to Han students. In addition to a free dormitory room, this subsidy covered food, books, stationary, haircuts, entry to a public bath, recreation, and other miscellaneous expenses.

Gone was the ten-year trend to reduce the number of hours in Korean-language studies. The movement toward ethnically mixed schools was reversed. As of 1979, Yanbian had 475 single-ethnic primary and middle schools and about 200 ethnically mixed schools. The proportion of single-ethnic schools did not reach the pre-Cultural Revolution level (90 percent in 1965), but more of them have been reorganized in recent years. Ethnically mixed schools were maintained in those areas where a mixture of different ethnic groups existed or where it was difficult to manage single-ethnic schools in rural districts. Twenty-nine schools in Yanbian were designated "key schools," receiving priority in educational programs and funding decisions. They included 8 Korean primary schools and 6 Korean middle schools. In a conscious attempt to correct the "abnormal phenomenon" of Korean students entering Han Chinese schools, the Yanbian government initially devised a quota system in 1979: the number of Korean students enrolled in Han Chinese schools should not exceed 10 percent in each grade for primary schools and 20 percent in each grade for middle schools.[9] This quota system was subsequently relaxed, but Korean students needed higher test scores than Han students to enter Han schools. "Otherwise," a Yanbian educator explained, "Korean students may dominate Han schools."

108

In 1985 only 0.7% of Korean children attended the Han Chinese primary schools in Yanbian and the corresponding figure was 12.7% in Han Chinese middle schools.[10]

For higher education in Yanbian, Yanbian Medical College and Yanbian Agricultural College were reopened in the mid-1970s. Faculty members in xiafang status were brought back to campus. Yanbian University restored the independence of its Department of Korean Language and Literature and increased the quota for Korean student admissions. Since some Korean undergraduate students (up to 15 percent in 1981), notably those who had attended Korean senior middle schools, had difficulty in understanding lectures or taking notes in Chinese, Yanbian University taught required courses in both Chinese and Korean and held special review sessions for Korean students in difficult subjects (such as Ancient Chinese History).

By 1979, the Yanbian government reinstated 1,247 teachers who were victims of the Cultural Revolution and exonorated 526 teachers who had been erroneously labeled "rightwing elements."[11] Particular attention was paid to restoring and strengthening normal schools. Although 11,000 Korean teachers taught in Korean primary and secondary schools in 1979, there was an acute shortage of competent Korean teachers in Yanbian. About 30 percent of the primary school teachers in Yanbian graduated from normal schools during the Cultural Revolution. They required a great deal of additional on-the-job training, special workshops and institutes, or correspondence courses. Only 27.6

percent of the Korean middle school teachers completed regular college programs.[12] In Heilongjiang Province 30.9 percent of the 2,100 Korean middle school teachers graduated from colleges, and 43.8 percent of the 3,200 Korean primary school teachers completed normal schools or senior middle schools, others graduated from junior middle schools.[13] A Korean-language educational journal, Yonbyon Kyoyuk [Yanbian Education], was reinstated to facilitate the exchange of useful information among Korean teachers. The November 1979 issue included a report by the Yanbian Education Bureau, an explanation of the Rules of Primary School Students, an editorial on physical education and public health, and 13 articles on teaching experiences, methods, and lessons. Other segments included a report by a Yanbian University history professor who graded the college entrance examination in Korean, 2 reports by teachers who graded the senior middle school entrance examinations in Korean, a Chinese-language article on curriculum in Chinese, a Korean song, and a report on North Korea which was a translation from Renmin Ribao.

Another important task in minority education was to increase the quantity and quality of textbooks originally written in minority languages. The Yanbian Education Bureau announced a 3-year plan (1978-1980) to accelerate the publication of Korean textbooks and other reading material; 400 new titles were issued in 1980 alone. The Yanbian books are widely used by Korean students all over the Northeast. Kang Yong-dok points out the limited availability of extra-curricular

110

reading material in the Korean language. According to a survey conducted in April 1980, the amount of extra-curricular reading material which Korean students in a key primary school of Yanjin City read a year was 37 percent of what their Han Chinese counterparts read in a key primary school of Changchun City.[14] The corresponding amount for Korean middle school students was only 25 percent. He implies that in terms of reading experience Korean students cannot compete well with their Han Chinese peers.

The ethnically-based educational system for Koreans in Yanbian and other parts of China's northeastern region was revived in the post-Cultural Revolution era. It was proudly reported that in 1980 the total number of students in Yanbian reached about 506,700--22.3 percent of Yanbian's total population.[15] The report said that the number of schools in 1980 increased 2.3 times over the 1949 level, the size of the entire student body increased 3.3 times, the number of educational staff increased 6.7 times, and the number of teachers (30,684) increased 5.7 times. It added that about 74,000 workers and peasants in Yanbian pursued their sparetime study programs in 1,919 locations at primary, secondary, and college levels.

The overall political framework for Yanbian's Korean educational programs was assured by the steady ascendancy of Korean political and educational leaders and by the increase in educational expenditures. After Choe Hae-ryong's downfall in 1977, Cho Nam-ki (Zhao Nanqi) took over the Yanbian CCP Committee as its First Secretary until 1983. A leader of the Yanbian Military

Unit (and a veteran of the Korean War), he assumed a number of local, provincial, and national political roles. He was a Deputy to the Fifth and Sixth National People's Congress (in 1979 and 1983), Vice Chairman of the NPC's Nationalities Committee (in 1980), Vice Governor of Jilin Province (in 1980), and Regular Member of the 12th CCP Central Committee (in 1982). In 1983 he moved from Yanbian to Changchun as a Secretary of the Jilin Provincial CCP Committee and Political Commissar of the Jilin Military District; in 1985 he went to Beijing as Senior Deputy Director of the General Logistics Department (under Director Hong Xuezhi) in the Chinese People's Liberation Army. His rapid rise in political leadership is in part attributable to his flawless competence in the Chinese language. Another Korean leader, Cho Ryong-ho (Cao Longhao), headed the Yanbian People's Government between 1979 and 1982; he was a member of the Standing Committee of the 6th National People's Congress. A longtime Yanbian cadre, Choe Lim (Cui Lin) replaced Cho as Yanbian's Chief Administrator and Second CCP Secretary in 1982, but he soon stepped down due to illness. In 1984, Li Tok-su (Li Deshu), a 40-year old graduate of Yanbian University, held several top positions in Yanbian--Chief Administrator, First CCP Secretary, and Political Commissar of the Yanbian Military Unit; in 1985 he relinquished the Chief Administrator position to another Korean--Hwang Chae-lim (Huang Zailin). Li was elected as an Alternate Member of the CCP Central Committee in September 1985. In the Yanbian People's Government there were 5 Deputy

Administrators in 1984--three Han Chinese (Mao Ruiting, Zhang Guoqin, and Sun Hongxiang) and two Koreans--Ra Chang-jin (Lu Changzhen) and Kim Chin-gom (Jin Zhengqian). Another Korean leader--Kim Tong-qi (Jin Dongji)--was the powerful Secretary-General of the Yanbian People's Government in 1984, but he became a Deputy Administrator in 1985. He was primarily responsible for the development of Yanbian's economic relations with China's other areas as well as foreign countries. While Cho Ryong-ho served as the Chairman of the Yanbian Prefectural People's Congress, a veteran Han leader, Tian Renyong, was the Chairman of the Yanbian Committee of the Chinese People's Political Consultative Conference. Tian was an officer in the New Fourth Army (led by Li Xiannian) during the anti-Japanese War and came to Yanbian in 1946. Since then he has been one of the key Han leaders in Yanbian. He is fluent in Korean and has a Korean wife. His warm personality, modest mannerisms, and quick smile contribute to his immense popularity among Koreans. He characterizes the Koreans as highly educated, progressive, and adaptive and refers to the Han-Korean relationship in Yanbian as excellent.[16] He says that as a result of their very strong "educational zeal," the Korean minority produced many college professors. Other Korean leaders in Jilin Province included Choe Chae (Cui Cai; ex-Deputy Administrator of Yanbian; and Vice Chairman of the Standing Committee of the Jilin Provincial People's Congress), Kim Myong-han (Jin Minghan; ex-Alternate Member of the 11th CCP Central Committee; ex-Deputy to the Fifth National People's

Congress; and Vice Chairman of the Jilin Provincial Committee of the Fifth Chinese People's Political Consultative Conference), and Hyon Yun-hi (Xuan Yunji) (ex-Director of Higher Education in the Jilin Provincial Department of Education).

The Yanbian Korean leadership paid special attention to educational programs in their budgetary decisions. <u>Renmin Ribao</u> noted that Yanbian's educational expenditures in 1982 showed a 96 percent increase over those in 1978 and that the budget for basic educational construction grew 2.4 times during this 5-year period. It also favorably reported that educational costs amounted to 15.9 percent of Yanbian's total local government budget in 1978 and 20.6 percent in 1982.[17] The corresponding figures in 1979 and 1980 were 15.8 percent (16,398,591 yuan) and 19.7 percent (23,286,000 yuan), respectively. Professor Tsurutani Setsure, who visited Yanbian in 1976, noted that Yanbian received a "budget for education which is three times higher than that allocated to Han areas". According to him, this funding was needed to prepare Korean-language textbooks and bilingual instructional programs.[18] Yet in 1982, Kim Song-ok (Yanbian CCP Deputy Secretary) mentioned that educational expenditures were still "too low" in Yanbian and reminded his audience that heavy educational investment led to a rapid pace of scientific and economic development in Japan and the Soviet Union.[19] He suggested that since the central government, because of its own economic difficulties, was not in a position to increase its educational subsidies rapidly, Yanbian

114

must bear a greater degree of financial responsibility for educational advancement.

<u>Primary and Secondary Education</u>

Traditionally, mothers and grandparents took care of pre-school children at home. As mothers were liberated from home to take part in productive activities during the time of agricultural mutual aid teams, Yanbian opened an initial educational program for pre-school children in 1947. In 1951, it established the first kindergarten (named "June First") at Yanji City and opened a school for kindergarten teachers. In 1980 kindergartens were available throughout Yanbian--1,743 classes in 881 kindergartens with 39,700 children (age 5 to 7), who were taught by 2,454 teachers.[20] Nine hundred and ten classes were attached to primary schools. There were 220 kindergarteners per 10,000 population in Yanbian, much higher than the national average (about 105). The curriculum at Korean kindergartens was designed to expose the child at an early age to Korean songs, dances, and customs. It was reported in 1983 that about 41 percent of eligible pre-school children attended kindergartens in Yanbian.[21] In Helong and Yanji Counties with a large number of Korean inhabitants, the proportion was much higher. Helong County was nationally recognized as one of the most advanced communities in kindergarten education; it is often visited by outsiders.

Primary schools were almost universally accessible in Yanbian as early as 1952; about 85 percent of school-age children studied at 577 primary schools at that time. The percentage was higher among Korean children (over 90 percent) than among their Han Chinese counterparts. Compared with the situation in 1952, by 1980 the number of primary schools (1,300) increased 2.25 times; the number of students (275,800) more than doubled; and the number of teaching staff (13,300) increased 1.6 times. The proportion of primary school teachers who graduated from senior middle schools or above was 64.9 percent, and 48.5 percent of middle school teachers graduated from colleges or specialized senior middle schools, such as normal schools.[22] Nearly 98 percent of all school-age children in Yanbian entered primary schools in 1981. While the number of China's total primary school students per 10,000 population was 1,428 in 1981 and the figure among minority nationalities was 1,094, the corresponding number in Yanbian (1,520) was higher than both figures.

However, Yanbian Deputy Administrator Sun Hongxiang (Han) candidly pointed to several problems faced by primary educational programs in Yanbian: (1) some cadres who are not fully cognizant of the importance of primary education, are stingy in educational investments; (2) school administration is not always rational; (3) the quality of Yanbian's educational programs has not improved as fast as in other parts of Jilin Province; (4) educational programs are not modernized; and (5) teachers continue to have difficulty in securing housing accommodation, admission to the Chinese Communist Party, and employment opportunities for their children. He urged educators in Yanbian to follow CCP General Secretary Hu Yaobang's

116

instructions to produce good minority human resources.[23] It is also pointed out that some school facilities are dilapidated and that library holdings are less than one book per primary school student in Yanbian.[24]

The secondary educational system in Yanbian, as elsewhere, is divided into three categories of schools--regular middle schools (junior middle schools and senior middle schools), specialized middle schools (technical middle schools and normal middle schools), and agricultural and vocational middle schools. A number of privately operated junior middle schools sprung up in the immediate postwar period, but they all became public schools in 1950. In 1958, 90 percent of primary school graduates entered junior middle schools in Yanbian as a whole; over 95 percent did so in Yanji City and Helong and Hunchun Counties. In 1983, the proportion reached 93.1 percent in Yanbian, and 46.6 percent of junior middle school graduates advanced to senior middle schools.[25] In Heilangjiang Province 87.4% of Korean primary school graduates advanced to junior high schools.[26]

In 1980 Yanbian had a total of 241 regular middle schools with 191,330 students (137,420 in 3-year junior middle schools and 53,910 in 2-3 year senior middle schools). About 47 percent of middle school students were Koreans. There were 13,980 educational staff (teachers, administrators, and support personnel). Compared with 1949, the number of regular middle schools in Yanbian grew 6.7 times by 1980; the comparable growth rates were 12.1 times in the size of total enrollment and 26.6 times in the number of educational staff members. According to Professor Kanno Hiroomi of Tokyo University of Foreign Studies, who visited Yanbian in 1981, about 90 percent of Korean primary school graduates entered junior middle schools and about 57 percent of Korean lower middle school graduates advanced to senior middle schools. The proportion of all middle school students was about 1,055 per 10,000 population in Yanbian; the number of Korean middle school students was 1,214 per 10,000 Koreans in Yanbian. The two figures were substantially higher than the national average (484), the average (263) for all minority nationalities, and even the average (880) in Jilin Province. For four years (1977- 1980), 4,406 graduates of Yanbian's senior middle schools were admitted to institutions (colleges and institutes) of higher education; 60.4 percent (2,661) of them were ethnic Koreans. In 1980, only 3.7 percent of Yanbian's total higher middle school graduates passed the tough college entrance examinations; the national average was 3 to 4 percent.

According to President Pak Mun-il of Yanbian University, the number of Yanbian Korean students who passed the extremely competitive college entrance examinations increased every year--812 in 1982, 920 in 1983, and 977 in 1984.[27]

In this connection, Pak Tu-hi, Principal of the First Yanbian Middle School (FYMS) in Yanji City, which admits the best Korean students throughout Yanbian, proudly stated that about 80 percent of FYMS graduates passed the college entrance examinations every year and that the most outstanding students moved to Beijing, Qinghua, Nankai, Fudan, Zhongshan, Shanghai Jiaotong, and other prestigeous universities.[28] In 1982, for example, 106 out of 283 FYMS graduates entered China's key universities and 112 persons joined other institutions of higher learning. In the best Han Chinese school (the Second Yanbian Middle School) in Yanbian, only 50 percent of the graduates entered colleges. The FYMS was established as a senior middle school in November 1952 under Prncipal Yun Tong-su (a veteran cadre from Yanan), but it included a junior middle school in 1982. In 1958 it was designated as a key school in Jilin Province; between 1952 and 1965, it educated 3,660 graduates, over 70% of whom entered colleges.[29] In 1978-1979, the Ministry of Education in Beijing included FYMS in the list of 20 national key schools in primary and secondary education; it was the only minority school so honored. Subsequently it was designated as one of 24 key middle schools in Jilin Province; again, it was the only minority school included in this exclusive club. Principal Pak, an able and dedicated educator, explained that FYMS, as a key school, had three major characteristics. First, it was a model to be studied and followed by other schools. Second, it was an experimental school where innovative curricula and new ideas were tested. Third, it was a central high-quality educational unit which received special consideration in educational budgets, qualified faculty, and modern equipment and facilities. In 1984 85 percent of its faculty were college graduates; over 70% of its faculty taught more than 20 years following their college graduation. The average number of college-trained faculty was only 27.6 percent in all of Yanbian's middle schools. The Han key schools had 4 faculty per class, but the FYMS was given additional faculty (0.25 per class) because it required additional staff to teach the Chinese and Korean languages.

In 1984, FYMS had 90 faculty and 950 students--16 senior middle school classes and 6 junior middle school classes. The principal medium of all instruction was Korean except for the two special senior classes taught in Chinese, which were phased out by July 1984. Each week students study the Chinese language for 5 hours; they study the Korean language for 4 hours during junior middle school years and 3 hours during senior middle school years. The content of textbooks on Korean language and literature included 75 percent translated materials and 25 percent originally written by Korean authors. Principal Pak said that a decision was made to make indigenous Korean writings comprise up to 75 percent of the contents of a textbook, but frankly admitted that the quality of such textbooks might suffer because it was difficult to choose from the limited number of high-quality indigenous Korean writings. The total weekly curriculum for Korean students had 3 or 4 more hours than that for Han students. It is therefore a considerable academic burden shared by all Korean students. As a principal foreign language, FYMS emphasized Japanese language at the cost of English. However, Principal Pak said that in view of the growing importance of English, his

120

school decided to teach English instead of Japanese to all freshmen students in 1984.

In addition to their remarkable performance in college entrance examinations, students at FYMS have shown an outstanding record of achievements in national and regional academic contests. In 1982, for example, an FYMS student received the highest score in a nation-wide mathematics contest and another student wrote the best essay in Jilin Province's history competition. In 1984 an FYMS representative ranked first in provincial mathematics examinations. In 1981 another student obtained the most points in national contests in the Japanese language. The FYMS also enjoys a high national reputation in soccer and wrestling.[30]

The First Tumen Middle School, another Korean institution, could not switch from Japanese to English because it had no English teacher. Situated near the Chinese-North Korean border, it still used an old wornout building which had belonged to a Branch Office of the Japanese Consulate-General. Unlike FYMS, it did not have a junior middle school; it had 4 classes for each of the three levels in a senior middle school. According to Principal Li Pyong-hak, 32 percent of its graduating seniors passed the college entrance examinations in 1984.[31] Students studied the Korean language for 4 hours, Chinese for 5 hours, and Japanese for 5 hours (Table 5.3). He explained that his daughter attended a Han primary school because they used to live in a Han Chinese community. He said that his school had some cultural exchange programs with North Korea across the Tumen River. In the summer students can no

TABLE 5.3

Curriculum for Korean Students in Yanbian:
Studies in Korean and Chinese Languages, 1981

(hours per week)

	Korean Language	Chinese Language
Primary School:		
First Grade	13	0
Second to Fifth Grades	8-9	6
Junior Middle School:		
First and Second Grades	4	6
Third Grade	4	5
Senior Middle School:		
First Grade	3	6
Second and Third Grades	3	5

Source: Kanno Hiroomi's report in Chosen Gakuho [Korean Studies Review] (April 1983).

122

longer swim or fish in the Tumen River because it is thickly polluted by industrial plants on both sides of the border river.

A former Korean student of the Second Yanbian Middle School--the best Han Chinese institution in Yanbian--says that when he graduated from a Korean primary school, it recommended the two best Korean students, including him, to enter the Second Yanbian Middle School (SYMS). He remembers that his Han Chinese classmates treated him well and that he felt free to use the Korean language with other Korean schoolmates. According to him, some Han Chinese students called him "gaoli fangzi" on a few rare occasions. Although he continued to use Korean at home and with his Korean friends, he soon became more comfortable with the Chinese language in reading and writing. As a result, he was psychologically constrained in using the Korean language publicly because he was afraid of making mistakes. In 1977 he took the nation-wide college entrance examination in the Chinese language and was able to enter Beijing Unversity. He explains that upon his graduation from Beijing University, he volunteered to return to Yanbian because he wanted to be close to his aging parents and that he started re-learning the Korean language. Another Korean graduate of SYMS says that his thorough familiarity with the Chinese language was quite useful for his medical training at the Norman Bethune Medical College in Changchun.

In 1949, Yanbian had one specialized middle school--the Yanbian Normal School which had 736 students and 29 educational staff; all of them were Koreans. By 1980, there were 7 specialized middle schools which students usually entered upon graduation from junior middle schools. They were Yanbian Normal School (which trained Korean students to teach in Korean), Yanbian Chinese-Language Normal School (which trained students--both Korean and Han Chinese--to teach in Chinese), Dunhua Normal School, and four technical middle schools--fine arts, public health, physical education, and finance and trade. The Yanbian School of Fine Arts was open only to Korean students and emphasized traditional Korean art, music, and dance, but the other three schools were ethnically integrated. Established in 1957, the Yanbian School of Fine Arts (headed by Principal Kim Sam-jin) had 314 students and 160 teaching and staff members in 1985.[32] Except for three Han Chinese (two teachers and one staff member), all were Koreans. It recruited some young students of musical instruments directly from primary schools and sometimes accepted junior middle school students interested in dance. In 1983 it also opened the college-level Department of Fine Arts in cooperation with Yanbian University. The curriculum was designed to teach students how to use Korean musical instruments such as the Kayagum and Chango (drum) and to dance in distinctly Korean styles and costumes. The techniques of painting were heavily influenced by Western art, but they almost exclusively painted Korean subjects. The school was planning to send an 18-member song-and-dance troupe to the United States at the invitation of Korean community organizations.

In a four year period (1977-1980), 5,987 students passed the entrance examinations to the seven specialized middle schools; 49.1 percent of them were Koreans. In 1980, these schools had 2,461 students and 794 educational staff members, an increase of 2.3 times and 26 times, respectively, over the numbers in 1949. In 1982, the Yanbian Normal School and the Yanbian Chinese Language Normal School were merged into the First Yanbian Normal School. It was expected to have 720 Korean students in 19 classes in the next few years.[33] Yanbian had 15 agricultural middle schools and 4 vocational middle schools, which were administered by the city and county governments, not the Yanbian Prefectural People's Government.

Higher Education

As discussed earlier, Yanbian University in Yanji City started as the Northeast Korean People's University in 1949 with 490 students and 60 teachers and administrative staff. By 1983 it had graduated 7,061 persons in regular undergraduate and graduate programs and 826 persons in correspondence courses; 70 percent of them were Koreans.[34] They constituted a core of Korean teachers and cadres who assumed positions of leadership in many fields, especially education and culture. In 1980, Yanbian University had 1,480 students; 65 percent were Koreans (Table 5.4). It also had 27 graduate students (yanjiusheng). The number of students surpassed the pre-Cultural Revolution level (1,200). The student body increased to 1,900 undergraduate students and 35 graduate students in 1984.[35] The university's educational staff

TABLE 5.4

Colleges in Yanbian, 1980

	Students			Educational Staff		
	Total Number	Koreans	%Koreans	Total Number	Koreans	%Koreans
Yanbian University	1,480	962	65	836	643	77
Uanbian Medical College	877	342	39	473	326	69
Yanbian Agricultural College	799	343	43	633	563	89
Yanbian Normal College	391	NI[a]	NI[a]	NI[a]	NI[a]	NI[a]

Source: Yanbian chaoxianzu zizhizhou gaikuang [The General Situation of the Yanbian Korean Autonomous Prefecture] (1982).

[a]No information.

embraced 848 persons, including 47 Full and Associate Professors and 249 Lecturers; 77 percent were Koreans. About 40 additional faculty were promoted to the ranks of Associate Professor toward the end of 1984. According to Professor Li Hwi-il (Li Xiyi), 75 percent of the faculty members were Koreans and 80 percent of these Korean faculty members graduated from Yanbian University. On the advantages of having Yanbian's Korean graduates as teaching staff, he maintained, "they have a thorough familiarity with and close feeling toward their alma mater and can devote themselves to enriching and developing the cultural and educational work for their own nationality."[36] However, he said, it was necessary for Yanbian University to hire and produce a certain number of Han Chinese faculty members who would enhance the standards and quality of higher education in a frontier area. One gnawing problem was the fact that some Han Chinese faculty members felt isolated in a predominently Korean environment and wanted to transfer to other Chinese colleges.

Since its inception, the presidency of Yanbian University has been assumed by Koreans; Chu Tok-hae (1949-1966), Pak Kyu-chan (Piao Kuican, 1978-1983), and Pak Mun-il (Piao Wenyi, 1983-). In spite of his diverse political roles (Chief Administrator in Yanbian, Alternate Member of the CCP Central Committee, Deputy to the National People's Congress, and Vice Governor of Jilin Province), Chu devoted much of his attention to Yanbian University on the assumption that it was essential to produce a sufficient number of competent Korean cadres. In 1962 President Chu brought Li Hwi-il from Changchun to be the First CCP Secretary of Yanbian University; born in Bongwha, North Kyongsang Province, Li Hwi-il immigrated to Manchuria at age 11. As a quiet but widely respected leader, Professor Li chaired the Chinese Association of Korean Language and was a Deputy to the Chinese People's Political Consultative Conference. He attended a conference on Korean Linguistics at Tokyo in 1983. Pak Kyu-chan, a mild-mannered and soft-spoken gentleman, joined Yanbian University in 1949 and was appointed Vice President in 1955 and then President in 1978. He was a specialist in political economy. He was succeeded by one of his disciples, Pak Mun-il, in 1983.

Pak Mun-il was born in Longjing in 1932; he attended Haesong Primary School and Tonghong Middle School in his native city. In 1949 he entered Yanbian University with a major in Chinese and Korean History. He was a Deputy Director of the Yanbian Institute of History and Language in the early 1960s; he spent 3 years on a farm during the Cultural Revolution. An articulate, sophisticated, and ambitious intellectual, he headed the Yanbian Historical Research Institute for several years. In addition to his administrative duties, he is the President of the Chinese Association of Korean History, a Director of the Chinese Historical Association, a Deputy to the 6th National People's Congress, and the First CCP Secretary of Yanbian University. He edited <u>Ryoksa Sajon</u> [Historical Dictionary] (published by the Yanbian People's Publishing House in 1984), which is a standard

128

reference book for Korean students in China. He espouses a long-range vision to promote Yanbian University's open-door policy toward advanced foreign educational institutions, especially in the United States; for this reason he visited several American universities in 1984. President Pak is assisted by First Vice President Chong Pan-ryong (Zheng Panlong) and two other Vice Presidents--a Korean (Kim Chong-chon) and a Han Chinese (Wang Jiaxing). A native of Kwangju, South Cholla Province, Chong studied in the Soviet Union and Sweden. He has a very sociable personality and a pragmatic cosmopolitan outlook. He is the President of the Chinese Association of Korean Literature. In 1985 he joined Professor Chae-Jin Lee in signing the academic exchange agreement between Yanbian University and the University of Kansas; it was the first such agreement concluded with a U.S. institution. Vice President Kim graduated from the Longjing Middle School and Yanbian University and studied at Kumamoto University in the early 1980s. A noted organic chemist, he visited the United States in 1985. Vice President Wang, a former military officer, was a political appointee with no academic background. He was primarily responsible for the University's finance, construction, maintenance, and service functions.

In 1980, Yanbian University had 8 divisions (hakbu or xi)--Languages and Literatures, Foreign Languages, Politics, History, Mathematics, Chemistry, Physics, and Physical Education--and offered 11 specializations (chuanye). It established a Division of Fine Arts in

1983 and a Division of Engineering in 1984; it planned to add Law, Economic Management, Machine-Building, Architecture, Electronic Technology, and Geography. The Division of Languages and Literatures embraced three departments--Korean Language and Literature, Chinese Language, and Chinese Literature. Professor Choe Yun-gap chaired the Department of Korean Language and Literature; as a specialist of Korean linguistics, he attended an international conferences at Tokyo in 1983. Headed by Professor Kim Yong-mun (a former newspaper editor) and Professor Wang Yu (Vice President Chong's Chinese wife), the Division of Foreign Languages offered Japanese, English, and Russian, and its Department of Japanese Language is known to be especially strong. Professor Kanno Hiroomi, who observed classes in Japanese literature at Yanbian University, reports that the level of practical Japanese language used by students was "extremely high" and that the Yanbian television station features a very good program in Japanese langauge study.[37] In 1985 Professor Omura Masuo of Waseda University, a specialist in Korean literature, began his two-year visiting position at Yanbian University to teach courses in Japanese literature. The Department of English was opened in 1983. For the first time in Yanbian's history, a Chinese-American lady came to the university in 1984 to teach English. She taught both students and a small group of selected faculty members who were planning to study in the United States. In addition, a Korean-American teacher and his American wife were expected to teach English at Yanbian

University in 1985. Yanbian University has sent a small number of its graduates and teachers to North Korea, Japan, the Soviet Union, and, most recently, Sweden. For example, a Yanbian University graduate (Choe Ung-gu), who studied at Kim Il-song University for a few years, is now an Associate Professor of Korean Literature at Beijing University. Fluent in Japanese, he was a visiting professor at Tokyo University of Foreign Studies during the 1983-84 academic year. Each year one or two Yanbian University faculty members visit Kim Il-song University for short-term research in Korean literature and history. Under President Pak's aegis, a number of U.S. institutions of higher learning are expected to attract an increasing number of Yanbian University faculty members and post-graduate students.

Even though the overall quality of Yanbian University is not at all comparable to China's major national universities or Jilin University at Changchun, it prides itself as being the oldest minority university in China. It is probably one of the most advanced institutions among China's 68 minority colleges, including 11 nationalities institutes. In particular, Yanbian University enjoys a solid national reputation in Korean Studies, Chemistry, and Japanese Philosophy. A Korean lecturer at Beijing University claimed that Yanbian University was superior to the Central Nationalities Institute in Beijing. In 1981, the Central Nationalities Institute had 14 Korean teaching staff, 82 Korean students specializing in Korean studies, and an additional 40 Korean students in other academic programs. However, a Yanbian University professor said that Inner Mongolian University was catching up with his school due to a difference in funding conditions. While Inner Mongolian University, directly under the Ministry of Education, obtained a substantial amount of central budgetary support, Yanbian University, under the Jilin Provincial Government, was less well-funded. Indeed, Professor Pak Kyu-chan expressed serious concern about the slow pace of Yanbian University's qualitative improvement vis-a-vis other minority institutions. He also pointed out that Yanbian University, which had assumed a primary interest in producing secondary school teachers, neglected economic, managerial, and technological subjects. He suggested that it must nurture at least one or two internationally recognizable professors in each department. New emphasis on English was cited as another practical step toward Yanbian University's internationalized curriculum. Furthermore, in order to recruit high-quality freshmen, President Pak Mun-il hopes that Yanbian University can move from second-round to first-round status in selecting college aspirants in Jilin Province.[38]

Yanbian University offers a five-year correspondence program for Korean teachers and cadres in other parts of China, mostly in the Northeast. This popular outreach program attracted about 4,200 students by 1984, who studied the Korean Language, the Chinese Language, Chinese Literature, Politics, Mathematics, Physics, History, Chemistry, and Geography. In 1984 evening classes were offered for 120 non-traditional students in the Korean Language, Politics, and Physics.

Visiting Yanbian University in 1984 and 1985, I was impressed by a few new buildings on campus--the multi-story library, the modern gymnasium, and the high-rise engineering building. One old office and classroom complex, which had been a local headquarters of the Japanese Kwantung Army, was under repair. While the Jilin Provincial Government allocated a special fund for library construction, the Ministry of Education and the State Nationalities Affairs Commission jointly financed the gymnasium to encourage Korean students to excel in athletic achievements. President Pak admitted that Yanbian University's various construction projects were enthusiastically supported by top Korean leaders such as Mun Chong-il (Vice Minister of the State Nationalities Affairs Commission until 1982) in Beijing and Cho Nam-ki in Changchun. The library contained about 420,000 volumes in Korean, Chinese, Japanese, and other languages. It displayed recent issues of South Korean newspapers-- Donga Ilbo, Seoul Sinmun, and Hanguk Kyongjae Sinmun. Yanbian University has several research institutes--the Korean Research Institute (headed by Chu Hong-song), the Nationality Research Institute (headed by Kwon Chol), and the Archaeological Research Institute (headed by Ko Yong-il). Each institute has about 20 staff members. The university has research organizations in Japanese Studies, Higher Education, and Minority Education. Yanbian University also houses the home offices of the Chinese Associations of Korean

History, Korean Language, Korean Literature, and Japanese Philosophy. In addition, the Yanbian government itself maintains the Historical Research Institute (headed by Han Chun-gwang), the Language Research Institute, the Research Institute on Literature and Arts, and the Research Institute on Minority Education. In 1985 all four research institutes were placed under the new Yanbian Academy of Social Sciences headed by An Ung-sop (former Professor of Economics at Yanbian University).

The Yanbian Medical College in Yanji City had its origin in a small Japanese medical institute (established in 1940) at Longjing. In 1945, it was made a 50-student Medical Division of Yanbian University. Separated from Yanbian University in 1958, it expanded under President Choe Su-han except for the Cultural Revolution period. It trained about 4,070 medical staff by 1980. Although it was closed during much of the Cultural Revolution, it was reopened with a 2-year program in the mid-1970s; it now offers three specializations--a 5-year program in regular medicine, a 4-year program in pharmacy, and a 6-year program in special medicine with emphasis on Japanese-language curriculum. Administered by a Korean President (Kang Sun-gu), the college operates a 565-bed hospital and has two specialized training programs for nurses and laboratory technicians. The 5-year program has the last year and one post-graduate year set aside for clinical training. Thereafter, graduates practice medicine without any further examinations. About 200 hours of courses in Chinese medicine are given during

134

the 5-year educational period. The 6-year Japanese medical program started in 1979, and it has a small number of young and bright students (about 30 in 1984), equally divided between Koreans and Han Chinese. They spend their first year learning Japanese and then receive all instruction in Japanese. They also use Japanese-language textbooks edited by Yanbian Medical College faculty members; Japanese doctors are often invited to give special lectures. There are only two other such programs in the Northeast--at the Norman Bethune Medical College in Changchun and the Chinese Medical College in Shenyang. The Yanbian Medical College has developed a growing tie with some Korean-American doctors, such as Dr. Bong H. Hyun, Professor of Pathology at Rutgers Medical School and at Muhlenberg Hospital (Plainsfield, New Jersey). Dr. Hyun led several Korean-American medical delegations to Yanbian and invited Korean-Chinese doctors to the United States.[39]

In 1960 about two-thirds of the students were Koreans, but the proportion of Korean students decreased to 39 percent in 1980. Vice President Chong Pyong-jin explained in 1984 that about one half of the 948 students were Koreans; they enjoyed an advantage of 5 points added to their entrance examination scores.[40] About 80 percent of the faculty were Koreans. He added that Yanbian favorably compared with Beijing in terms of the number of medical doctors and hospital beds available per population size. In fact, there was an oversupply of Korean doctors and pharmacists in Yanbian, who were compelled to seek jobs away from

Yanbian. A graduate of Yanbian Medical College, who is now a deputy director of a university clinic in Tianjin, explains that her Yanbian medical education is no handicap in her practice.

The Yanbian Agricultural College in Longjing, another offshoot of Yanbian University, trained about 1,500 specialists in agriculture, forestry, and animal husbandry prior to the Cultural Revolution. Students from this college were instrumental in spreading and improving technical knowhow about rice production throughout the Northeast. Yanbian rice is so popular in China that it is often served at national banquets and state dinners in Beijing. In 1980, the college under President Pak Kyong-han had 799 students pursuing 4-year programs in Agronomy, Veterinary Medicine, and Agricultural Machinery. 43 percent of these students were Koreans. The educational staff numbered 633, 89 percent of whom were Koreans. According to Professor Chang Paek-lok, Yanbian Agricultural College has close ties with Hokkaido University in such fields as livestock breeding and artificial insemination. It also attempts to establish cooperative relations with the University of Georgia.

In addition to the three regular institutions of higher learning in Yanbian, there is Yanbian Normal College which offers 2-year training programs for teachers in five specializations--Mathematics, Chemistry, Physics, Chinese Literature, and English. In 1980, it had 391 students. Yanbian Educational College also exists to retrain middle school teachers and to do research on secondary education.

136

Programs for college-level sparetime education are widely available in Yanbian. In 1980 the Saebyok Sparetime Farmers' College was renamed the Saebyok Farmers' College. It had produced about 2,600 agricultural specialists in more than two decades. In 1980, it had 33 teaching staff (including 31 Koreans) and 157 students. All but 5 were Korean farmers. They pursued 3-year programs in agricultural science and animal husbandry. Another program is the Yanji Municipal Sparetime Workers' College. In 1980, it had about 170 students. Television is also used to teach college-level courses in Yanbian. When this program started in 1979, it enrolled about 400 students.

On the 30th anniversary of the Yanbian Korean Autonomous Prefecture in September 1982, Cho Nam-ki (Zhao Nanqi), the then First Secretary of the Yanbian Prefectural CCP Committee and Regular Member of the 12th CCP Central Committee, highlighted the progress of higher education as one of Yanbian's distinctive achievements. In his speech published in a Korean-language newspaper, Yonbyon Ilbo [Yanbian Daily], he said that the number of students attending Yanbian University, Yanbian Medical College, and Yanbian Agricultural College in 1981 was 3.5 times greater than that in 1952 and that there were 24.5 college students per 10,000 people in Yanbian.[41] He added that there were 33.2 Korean college students per 10,000 Koreans in Yanbian. The analysis of both figures suggests that the number of Han Chinese college students was less than 18.9 per 10,000 Han Chinese in Yanbian. At the Sixth National People's Congress in June 1983, Cho

Ryong-ho (Cao Longhao), former Chief Administrator of the Yanbian Prefecture, cited the same numbers (25 and 33) of students in Yanbian's "regular colleges."[42] And Renmin Ribao repeated the same information in August 1983.[43] Whatever numbers were used, there was little doubt that the number of Korean college students in Yanbian was larger than the national average in China (12.7 students per 10,000 people) and the average among China's minority nationalities (7.6 students per 10,000 minority population) in 1981. The Mongolians were the only other minority nationality whose college students (17 students per 10,000 Mongolians) were proportionally larger than the national average.[44] The comparable number for Xinjiang's minority nationalities was only 6.9. In 1984 President Pak Mun-il of Yanbian University said that 4,083 students attended Yanbian's three regular colleges and that 2,482 (60.8 percent) of them were Koreans.[45] He estimated that there were altogether about 8,000 Korean college students throughout China. These statistics represent an impressive manifestation of Koreans' determined pursuit of higher education in China.

NOTES

1. "Pyongang ui minjok kyoyuk paljon sikyo de manhon konsol injae lol yangsong hagetta" [We Will Nurture More Human Resources for Construction by Developing Ethnic Education in a Frontier Area], in Yonbyon Kyoyuk, Number 10 (1982), 40-41.

2. Yonbyon Kyoyuk, Number 3 (1982), 4.

3. Yonbyon Kyoyuk, Number 3 (1982), 7.

4. Renmin Ribao, December 7, 1982.

5. Beijing Review (November 17, 1980), 8.

6. Interview with Pak Kyu-chan, August 5, 1984, Yanji. See Su Wenming, ed., A Nation at School(Beijing: Beijing Review Publications, 1983), 49-56.

7. Zhongguo baike nianjian [Chinese Yearbook] (Beijing: Zhongguo baike nianjian chuanshu chubanshe, 1982), 380, and Guangming Ribao, March 29, 1982.

8. Pak Mun-il, "Chungguk yonbyon chosenjok ui munhwa kyoyuk paljon chonghyong" [The Conditions of Cultural and Educational Development of Yanbian's Korean Nationality in China] (unpublished paper, December 1984).

9. Yonbyon Kyoyuk, Number 3 (1979), 3.

10. Interview with Kang Yong-dok, August 9, 1985, Yanji.

11. Ibid., 6.

12. Yonbyon Kyoyuk, Number 9 (1982), 17-18.

13. Ibid., 19.

14. Kang Yong-dok, 12.

15. Yanbian gaikuang, 209-211.

16. Interview with Tian Renyong, August 6, 1984, Yanji.

17. Renmin Ribao, August 27, 1983.

18. Tsurushima, 104.

19. Yonbyon Kyoyuk, Number 12 (1982), 8-12.

20. Yanbian gaikuang, 215-216.

21. Yonbyon Kyoyuk, Number 6 (1984), 4.

22. Renmin Ribao, August 27, 1983.

23. Yonbyon Ilbo, August 4, 1984.

24. Yonbyon Kyoyuk, Number 7 (1984), 5.

25. Yonbyon Kyoyuk, Number 6 (1984), 4.

26. Ibid., Number 11 (1984), 5.

27. Pak Mun-il, "Chungguk yonbyon."

28. Interview with Pak Tu-hi, August 7, 1984, Yanji.

29. Yonbyon Kyoyuk, Number 10 (1984), 12-14 and 17.

30. Ibid., Number 10 (1984), 14.

31. Interview with Li Pyong-hak, August 7, 1984, Tumen.

32. Discussions with Kim Mun-mu and other teachers of the Yanbian School of Fine Arts, August 3, 1985, Yanji.

33. Yonbyon Kyoyuk, Number 9 (1982), 17-18.

34. Yonbyon Taehak [Yanbian University] (Beijing: Minzu chubanshe, 1984), 34-35.

35. Interview with Pak Mun-il, Li Hwi-il, and Chong Pan-ryong, August 4, 1984, Yanji.

36. Li Hwi-il (Li Xiyi), "Zongjie minzu jiaoyude jingyan jiaqiang yanbian daxue jianshe" [Summarize the Experience of Ethnic Education and Strengthen the Construction of Yanbian University], in Yanbian Daxue Xuebao, Numbers 1-2 (1981), 3.

37. Kanno Hiroomi, "Enben chosenzoku jichishu homon hokoku" [Report on the Visit to the Yanbian Korean Autonomous Prefecture], in Chosen Gakuho [Korean Studies Review] (Tokyo), Number 103 (April 1983), 91.

140

38. For the complicated rounds of college student selections, see Suzanne Pepper, China's Universities: Post-Mao Enrollment Policies and Their Impact on the Structure of Secondary Education(Ann Arbor: Center for Chinese Studies, University of Michigan, 1984), 83-105.

39. See Hyun Ung and Hyun Bong-hak, Chungkong ui hanindul [Koreans in China] (Seoul: Pomyangsa, 1984).

40. Interview with Chong Pyong-jin, August 6, 1984, Yanji.

41. Yonbyon Ilbo, September 3, 1982.

42. Renmin Ribao, June 10, 1983.

43. Renmin Ribao, August 27, 1983.

44. Beijing Review (October 7. 1983), 18.

45. Pak Mun-il, "Chungguk yonbyon."

6
Assessments and Conclusion

In spite of China's widely fluctuating minority policy over the years, the Koreans in China have tenaciously sustained a considerable range of ethnically oriented educational opportunities for their children in Yanbian and other parts of China's northeastern region. Even though it is difficult to assess the relative quality of the educational programs, the sheer quantity of Korean schools, students, and teachers is indeed remarkable, especially when compared with China's other minority nationalities. As suggested at the outset, there must be a variety of factors that can account for the reasonably successful records of the Korean educational experience in China.

First, as relative newcomers to China, they have inherited a strong cultural tradition and value system which invariably emphasizes education both for its intrinsic intellectual purpose and for its functional utility. Early Korean immigrants and settlers in China

141

were a mixture of poverty-stricken peasants, well-educated Confucian scholars, and modernized intellectuals, who were instrumental in transmitting the heritage of their homeland to their offspring in an alien environment. Second, the Koreans have jealously guarded their ethnic identity by protecting their language and social customs and discouraging intermarriage. Their natural propensity to organize their own communities and to nurture close personal networks is conducive to the maintenance of their ethnic and cultural self-identity. Third, unlike most of China's other minority nationalities, the Koreans benefit from their Confucian-influenced cultural background, which is essentially compatible with Han Chinese cultural patterns. Although the Korean phonetic alphabet, Hangul, is independent of Chinese ideographs, the Koreans have borrowed both Chinese characters and the Confucian classics for many centuries. Pronunciation is different, but a large number of Korean words may be written in Chinese characters. Most of the loan-words originally written in Chinese characters came from China, but some also came from Japan. Moreover, the Koreans do not have a dominant religious preference as do the Islamic minorities.

Fourth, it is very important to China's Korean minority that they have Yanbian as a territorial basis for ethnic identity and educational enrichment. The Yanbian Korean Autonomous Prefecture contains a little more than 40 percent of all the Koreans in China, but it serves as a cultural and psychological center which reaches out to other Korean communities. In a way, Yanbian sets a standard as well as an example of Korean educational programs and it publishes the bulk of Korean textbooks, periodicals, and reference materials available nationally. Added to the enormous advantages of Yanbian's existence is the favorable economic and cultural condition of China's northeastern region, which embraces more than 97 percent of the total Korean population in China. Compared with Xinjiang, Tibet, Inner Mongolia, Yunnan, Guangxi, and Guizhou where a large number of other minority nationalities live, the Northeast has highly developed industry, communications, education, and culture. The distinct geographic demarcations of the Northeast (or Manchuria) provide Koreans with a clearly identifiable boundary within which they live. They refer to themselves as residents of guanwai (outside Shanhaiguan Pass) as distinguished from those of guannei (inside Shanhaiguan Pass). The historic port city on the Sea of Bohai, Shanhaiguan in Hebei Province, where the Great Wall begins, has been used as a convenient point of separation between Manchuria and the rest of China.

Fifth, as Zong Qun suggested at the outset, the Koreans have taken advantage of the northeastern region's cultural and human infrastructure left by the Japanese colonial system. A vast number of Korean teachers in the immediate postwar period were educated in Japanese schools or in schools under Japanese influence. Likewise, one of the two meng that showed the highest rate of literacy among Mongolians in the 1950s had been under Japanese control in Manchukuo.[1]

Korean schools were built upon Japanese educational facilities. Korean intellectual leaders in their 50s and 60s are, for the most part, fluent in Japanese. Six out of 8 prominent Korean poets and writers identified in a directory of 99 minority literary figures in China acknowledged their association with Japanese educational influence. There were only three other persons to do so and they were all Mongolian authors (out of 20 Mongolians).[2] When I visited a Yanbian University professor at Tokyo hotel in 1983, he was reading the current issue of Sekai, a Japanese intellectual magazine. Almost all senior Korean faculty at Yanbian University, Yanbian Medical College, Yanbian Agricultural College, Jilin University, Beijing University, and other Chinese colleges are fluent in Japanese. They feel comfortable in dealing with Japanese visitors and Japanese-language materials. Early educational experience in Japanese is indeed a distinct advantage for those Koreans in China who are engaged in Japan-related affairs; a few examples are Chong Min (Minister-Counsellor at the Chinese Embassy in Japan), Kim So-song (ex-Counsellor at the Chinese Embassy in Japan), Yu Sin-sun (a productive scholar of Japanese diplomatic history at Nankai University), Chu Hong-song (a specialist of Japanese philosophy at Yanbian University), Han Yun-chol (Director of the Japan Bureau in the China International Travel Service), Pak Sae-hu (a special correspondent for Radio Beijing in Japan), Ro Min (ex-Director of the Asian Affairs Division in the Institute of Contemporary International Relations), and Choe Bin (a member of the

Asian and Pacific Affairs Division in the Institute of International Studies).

It is therefore no accident that Professor Kanno saw a solid Japanese language program at Yanbian University and that Yanbian Medical College can offer a special training program in Japanese. And the Yanbian Agricultural College is entrusted with the task of teaching Japanese to those Chinese agricultural specialists whom the Beijing government chooses to send to Japan. It is reported that a considerable number of Chinese exchange students in Japan are in fact Koreans, mostly from China's northeastern region. In Yanbian, a large majority of Korean middle school students take Japanese as a primary foreign language because teachers competent in Japanese are readily available and because it is relatively easy for Korean students to learn. However, the emphasis on Japanese in Yanbian leads to neglect of English in middle schools and colleges. According to Professor Pak Kyu-chan and Tian Renyong, this is a major weakness in Yanbian's foreign language programs.[3] Korean students who enter national universities suffer a disadvantage in learning English and using English-language materials. Therefore, the First Yanbian Middle School decided to introduce English, not Japanese, to its freshmen students in 1984.

Sixth, unlike other minority nationalities living in Xinjiang, Tibet, and Yunnan, the Koreans in China have received an appreciable degree of cultural influence from their ancestral homeland--mainly, North Korea which has a highly developed, though ideologically constrained, educational system. In the late 1940s, North Korean textbooks were widely used in Yanbian's Korean schools. This was a time when the Koreans on both sides of the Tumen River regarded Yanbian as an extension of North Korea. In the 1950s, educational exchange programs were established between China and North Korea. A number of North Korean scholars such as (Kim Su-gyong, Yu Yol, and Chong Yul-mo) visited Yanbian to advise on Korean language and literature, and Yanbian sent its teachers to study at North Korean colleges. A similar type of educational cooperation existed between Inner and Outer Mongolia in the 1950s.

Although North Korea's direct influence over Koreans' educational programs in China is no longer significant, its spillover effects are still unavoidable. The textbooks in Korean language and literature contain works written by North Korean authors such as Li Ki-yong and Choe Su-hae and are influenced by North Korean scholarship. Yanji City has a bookstore specializing in North Korean publications, and the foreign-language bookstores throughout the Northeast are well-stocked with books from North Korea. The Koreans in Yanbian can visit their relatives in North Korea with the travel permits issued by local governments; some North Koreans come to Yanbian, too. According to a Chinese border guard, about 150 persons cross the Tumen River Bridge every day in 1985. Since Kim Il-song and other North Korean leaders had their educational and revolutionary experience in China's northeastern region, there has been a certain degree of pro-Pyongyang sentiment among some Yanbian Koreans; this sentiment was reinforced during the Korean War. The cultural exchange programs between North Korea and Yanbian are active. In the first few days of August 1984, for example, Yanbian received three North Korean delegations--a youth musical troupe, a friendship group from Hoeryong, and an inspection team from North Hamgyong Province. In August 1985 I witnessed a greater number of North Korean delegations in Yanbian. Yanbian University has an agreement for the exchange of books with North Korean institutions, including Kim Il-song University, National Library, Central Science Library, People's Economic College, and the Great Hall of People's Study. North Korean radio and television programs are apparently accessible to Yanbian Koreans, and North Korean movies are said to be popular in Yanbian. A Yanbian native observed that North Korean films and television series such as "Flower Girl," "Chunhyangchon," and "Nameless Heroes" shown in China had a higher level of artistic quality than those of China. The two-volume Korean-language edition of Li Chin-u's "Nameless Heroes" published by the Yanbian People's Publishing House in 1982 is available at 3 yuan. The Korean language used in Yanbian is much influenced by North Korean terminology and pronunciation which are distinguishable from South Korean usage. Hence the spoken Korean of Yanbian students has three attributes--a strong North Hamgyong accent, North Korean terms and expressions, and Korean transliterations of Chinese characters. While Koreans in Liaoning Province tend to have a Pyongan accent,

148

many in Heilongjiang Province speak Kyongsang dialect. The efforts to eliminate the persistence of Korean regional dialects and to standardize the Korean language used in China have been ineffective.

South Korea's cultural penetration into China's Korean minority is limited, but is definitely growing. Some Koreans in China prefer to listen to Radio Seoul rather than Radio Pyongyang. An avid listener says that he particularly likes the soft Seoul accent used by female announcers and popular Korean music programs. Tapes of popular South Korean songs are readily available in Yanbian and widely used in dance parties. There has been a small-scale exchange of Korean family members between China and South Korea; Yanbian University professors (for example, Ko Chol and Min Yong-suk) and Korean authors (such as Chong Kil-un) visited Seoul in 1984. A few contemporary South Korean authors--such as Kim Chi-ha, Kim Tong-ni, O Yong-su, and Yom Sang-sop--have been introduced in Chinese publications such as Yanbian Daxue Xuebao [Yanbian University Journal], Arirang (a Korean literary magazine), and Munhak kwa Yaesul [Literature and Arts].[4] A collection of short stories written by about 20 South Korean writers was published in Shanghai. The Korean intellectuals in China have access to South Korean newspapers (such as Donga Ilbo) and magazines (such as Sin Donga and Chonggyong Munhwa). Yanbian University library has several thousand South Korean books recently imported via Japan. A Yanbian University professor commented that South Korean books were uniformly good in quality. An increasing number of South Korean universities, libraries, publishers, and cultural organizations (the Korean National Commission for UNESCO, the Korea Research Foundation, and the Daewoo Foundation) are eager to send a variety of newspapers, magazines, and books to Korean intellectuals in China. In 1985 Kim Wu-chung (Chairman of the powerful Daewoo Industrial Group), who secretly visited China himself, donated 3,000 Korean books to Yanbian University. As a result, a Yanbian University leader claimed, "Yanbian University can now boast its indisputable status as the best center for Korean Studies in China. We no longer have to go to Beijing to read South Korean books." And South Korean dictionaries and reference books are freely reproduced in Yanbian.

Needless to say, the combination of all six factors cited above is not sufficient to make the success of Korean minority educational programs possible unless it is supported by China's overall minority policy. If, for example, the ideologically-inspired radical integrationist policy exemplified by the Rectification Movement and the Cultural Revolution were sustained throughout the PRC era, it might have destroyed the underlying premises of identifiable education for minority nationalities. The presence of a national policy which recognizes the functional value of ethnic diversity and promotes an orderly and realistic accommodation of ethnically-oriented educational experiences seems to be a necessary condition for a viable minority educational system. On the other hand, no matter how enlightened or relaxed

China's minority policy might be, it would be difficult to transplant the Korean model of educational experience to other minority nationalities whose social characteristics are substantially dissimilar.

The educational system for the Korean minority nationality in China is not devoid of potentially serious problems and tensions. One of the most persistent pedagogical as well as practical issues is how to deal with the dilemma of bilingual education. While the Koreans in China prefer to assure that their children learn and use Korean, they are concerned that too much emphasis on Korean-language study may jeopardize or cripple their children's chances for upward social mobility·in the dominant Han cultural environment. It is the age-old tension between tradition-bound idealism and functionally-oriented pragmatism among China's minority nationalities. As Yonbyon Kyoyuk candidly admits, some Korean parents demand that their children be allowed to enter Han Chinese schools or to take more Chinese-language courses in Korean schools.[5] A Korean professor of the Central Nationalities Institute states that among some Korean families the Chinese language is viewed as a necessary means for a successful career. Similarly, upon his visit to a Korean production brigade in Jilin City, a New York Times reporter observed that "for all concessions to a Korean identity, fluency in Chinese offers the only sure hope of advancement."[6] Other parents suggest that their children in a key Korean middle school be admitted to a special class where all instructions are given in Chinese. In fact, all students in Korean schools except first-graders in primary schools are required to take 5 to 6 hours of Chinese-language courses a week. This requirement means that students in Korean schools have a total of more than 2,000 hours of Chinese-language courses until they graduate from senior middle schools. This obviously limits their ability to study other subjects and puts them in a disadvantageous position vis-a-vis their Han Chinese peers. Yet the average degree of competence in the Chinese language among the Korean senior middle school students is equal to that among the Han junior middle school students.[7] Furthermore, as Korean students take only four hours of Korean-language courses a week in junior middle schools and then three hours in senior middle schools, it is possible that they can excel ·in neither Korean nor Chinese. If a bright and ambitious senior student in a Korean senior middle school wishes to take the national college entrance examination in the Korean language, he must learn it well. If, however, he passes the examination and enters one of China's best national universities, he may have to struggle with his deficiency in Chinese. A Korean scholar points out that it is not easy for Korean students to switch specialized terminology (such as chemical symbols) and delicate nuances from Korean to Chinese. He says that Korean students retain a Korean accent in Chinese pronunciations.

A controversy surrounds the extent to which Yanbian University offers courses in Chinese and Korean languages. Some Korean professors are evidently

152

nostalgic about the pre-1958 system when all instruction was given in Korean. Since Yanbian University has Han Chinese students (35 percent) and Han faculty members (23 percent), it is unrealistic to revert to an all-Korean language curriculum. On the other hand, there are some Korean educators who emphatically argue that instruction in the Korean language must be upheld because "we cannot think of minority education without having minority language."[8] Kang Yong-dok contends that this principle is consistent with Marxist theory, the Chinese Constitution, and the Koreans' historical experiences. Another Korean scholar argues that unless one knows and uses his own national language, he cannot express his feelings and thoughts in a proper and effective fashion. Professor Li Hwi-il of Yanbian University proposes a method of dividing each department and each course (fenban fenke) into Korean-language and Chinese-language sections so that students can be competent in both languages.[9] A possible pitfall of this method is the virtual separation of students along lines of language preference. As the Korean language used in China is appreciably sinicized, Korean intellectual leaders tend to make conscious efforts to purify their language. For example, no Chinese characters are used in Korean textbooks, newspapers, and magazines. Streets and titles of magazines are named in indigenous Korean language--the names have no comparable Chinese characters. Examples of Korean-language magazines with indigenous titles are: Chindalle [Azalea], Onuyi [Brother and Sister], Dolgukhwa [Wild Camomile],

Bomnorae [Spring Song], Komabaksa [Child Doctor], Arirang, Mujigae [Rainbow], Saebyol [New Star], Sinaemul [Stream], Saemaul [New Village], Kotbaguni [Flower Basket], and Toraji [Balloon Flower]. Other Korean-language literary magazines whose titles can be transliterated into Chinese include Chonji [Heavenly Lake] (formerly Yonbyon Munye), Munhak kwa Yaesul [Literature and Arts], Saegye Munhak [World Literature], Changchun Munye [Changchun Literature], Kunjung Munye [Mass Literature], Unhasu [Milky Way], Changbaeksan [Changbaek Mountain], Haerangang [Haeran River], Songhwagang [Songhwa River], and Munhak Yesul Yongu [Study on Literature and Art].

Yet it is perhaps inevitable that in daily conversations educated Koreans use a mixture of Korean and Chinese expressions. The more distant they are from Yanbian, the more sinicized their conversations become. They borrow a large proportion of Chinese terms and phrases and mechanically pronounce them in Korean. For example, they say pirup (not chorup as used in Korea) for graduation (from biye in Chinese characters), aein (not puin) for wife (from airen), ryangman (not iman) for 2,000 (from liangwan), sajak (not chakmun) for composition (from xiezuo), konggu (not togu) for instrument (from gongju), kongin (not nodongja) for worker (from gongren), haegwan (not saegwan) for customs (from haiguan), and chaego (not hyangsang) for promotion (from tigao).

It is probably true that the Han Chinese people, who constitute a majority in Yanbian (58 percent), are supremely confident in their cultural superiority and do not feel threatened by their Korean neighbors. However, as Dreyer suggests, they may develop a sense of jealousy and competition or may resent the likelihood of reverse discrimination if any significant preferential treatment is given to Korean students in such specific areas as school admissions, educational funds, and job assignments.[10] In an attempt to reduce jealousy and friction between Korean and Han students, the educators in Yanbian have revived "friendship schools," "friendship classes," joint academic projects, and cooperative sports events between Korean and Han schools, which had been suspended during the Cultural Revolution.[11] The opportunities for college education are less widely available to the Han Chinese majority than to the Korean minority. And the Koreans enjoy a more active intellectual and cultural life than their Han Chinese countrymen do in Yanbian. As Cho Nam-ki points out, it is for historical reasons that the educational foundations for Han students are weak in Yanbian; Korean primary and middle schools have developed ahead of Han schools.[12] A majority of the Han Chinese were late-comers to Yanbian and were severely oppressed during the time of Japanese dominance. While visiting Yanbian, one gets the impression that the use of the Korean language is so prevalent that Han residents who do not know Korean may feel as though they were in a foreign country. Yet Han Chinese students rarely learn the Korean language. They do not pay much attention to the good radio programs in Korean-language studies or fine Korean-language textbooks published in Yanbian. A Yanbian

Korean educator expresses his genuine appreciation and warm feeling toward the few Han Chinese cadres in Yanbian, who made special efforts to acquire functional competence in the Korean language. The best case in point is Tian Renyong, the Chairman of the Yanbian Committee of the Chinese People's Political Consultative Conference. A Han Chinese teacher, who is assigned to a Korean middle school to teach the Chinese language, confesses that without knowledge of the Korean language it is very difficult to attend faculty meetings or to interact with Korean students. Although other frustrated Han Chinese teachers preferred to return to Han schools, he decided to learn the Korean language. He is now recognized as a "model of ethnic unity."[13]

The most serious concern that both Korean and Han parents have is not always associated with the relative linguistic emphasis of school curriculum, but it is rather closely related to whether or not their children can get into those schools designated as "key schools," irrespective of their ethnic makeup. This concern with educational elitism stems from the fact that since the key schools receive more funds and better facilities than non-key ones, students in key schools are more likely to advance to the institutions of higher education and thus to obtain prestigeous status and desirable employment.

In this context Cho Nam-ki deplored the fact that every Korean student wanted to enter a regular middle school and then to move to a college, while no more than 4 percent of the senior middle school graduates could be admitted to college.[14] According to him, this unrealistic expectation, which led to deemphasis on technical and vocational schools, was one of the main reasons why Yanbian enjoyed the highest level of educational and cultural achievements among the 6 prefectural units in Jilin Province, but had the lowest rate of development in technology and management. In 1981, Wang Enmao, the then First Secretary of the Jilin Provincial CCP Committee (and Deputy Commander of the Shenyang Military Region) also observed that Yanbian's industrial foundations were comparatively weak and that its economic development was slow.[15] Yanbian has a sufficient number of doctors, teachers, and agricultural and financial cadres, but lacks engineers, architects, managers, and electronics and textile specialists. The number of professional and technical school students per 10,000 population in Yanbian is only 7.7--much lower than the corresponding figures for Jilin Province (15.2) and China (10.7).[16] In fact, Table 6.1 shows that Yanbian's rate of industrial growth, labor productivity, and grain output lags far behind the average of the entire nation as well as Jilin Province. It is indeed a difficult challenge for Yanbian to implement a structural reform in its educational policy so that the present ratio (22.3 percent in 1983) of professional and technical schools among all middle schools can reach 50 percent in 1990 as prescribed by the Ministry of Education.

Another potentially gnawing consequence of educational elitism among Yanbian Koreans is an incipient sign of brain drain. The best graduates of

TABLE 6.1

Economic Conditions in Yanbian, 1981

	Yanbian Prefecture	Jilin Province	China
Population Density (per square km)	43	119	104
Per Capita Arable Land (in mu)	2.10	2.73	1.49
Per Capita Industrial Output (in yuan)	856	858	752
Per Capita Grain Output (in jin)	470	827	653
Labor Productivity (in yuan)	5.12	8.64	11.82
Rate of Industrial Growth (percent based on the 1952 figure)	480.8	1,408.8	1,962.7
Rate of Agricultural Growth (percent based on the 1952 figure)	222.1	222.9	270.7
Rate of Industrial and Agricultural Growth (percent based on the 1952 figure)	409.7	736.1	946.8

Source: Choe Ryong-hak's article in Yanbian Daxue Xuebao [Yanbian University Journal] (Special Edition in 1984).

158

key Korean senior middle schools are not likely to apply for Yanbian University or other local colleges, but they may aim at entering China's elite national or regional institutions of higher education. This desire is considerably facilitated by the fact that they can take the college entrance examinations in their native tongue. Once admitted to such Han institutions, their Korean educational background may not be a tangible asset, but probably a liability which they have to overcome. Their sense of ethnic identity may become beclouded in the Han Chinese cultural milieu except for their own social activities and mutual support networks. As one of them mentions in a letter, they may get good job assignments after graduation because of their minority status, but most of them may never return to Yanbian for career opportunities. Just before her college graduation, Miss Kim (whom I discussed in Chapter 5) wrote: "Now the only thing for me to do is to finish my graduation paper and to be assigned to a good job. Maybe the department leaders will show some special concern for us minorities." In another recent letter, she declared: "I would rather die than wait to be assigned to any unknown place. I want to work in Beijing because it is the cultural and economic center of our country and it is more civilized than other cities. Everything depends on it. I wish I would be very lucky in my assignment. May God bless me!" She continued: "Now I come to realize that living is not so easy and it is a hard struggle. If you want to have good status, you have to study hard and work hard. In addition to that, sometimes you must use your mind wisely. Anyway one should have confidence in oneself at all times." Miss Chang also says that she prefers to work in Beijing, but that she intends to return to her native Yanbian when she gets older. She feels that Yanbian University may not welcome her as a teacher. And, a successful Korean professor in China confesses that he always likes to visit Yanbian because of its natural beauty and his childhood memories, but he does not want to live there because life in a compact Korean community is too tense and complicated.

Since Yanbian University tends to hire its own graduates as faculty members, it is less than enthusiastic in recruiting the Korean graduates of the national and regional universities. Conversely, however, it supplies some of its best graduates, especially those in Korean Language and Literature, to other colleges and research institutes in China. I have met several Yanbian University graduates as faculty or researchers at Beijing University, the Central Nationalities Institute, and the Institute of Contemporary International Relations under the Chinese State Council. Yanbian Medical College and Yanbian Agricultural College also export their graduates to other places. The brain drain is still small in number, and it does not seem to be a cause of concern to Yanbian's Korean leaders and educators. If, however, it is significantly accelerated, Yanbian may be deprived of the services of its most capable sons and daughters in the long run. The return of Yanbian's best educated Koreans to their native communities will be particularly useful to its educational and cultural programs because Yanbian, due to its geographical isolation and political sensitivity, does not have easy access to the benefits of international educational exchanges. In comparison, Inner Mongolia and Xinjiang appear to be less restrictive in contacts with foreign schools and scholars. In 1981 Professor Kanno found Yanbian Koreans more isolated than their peers in Heilongjiang and Liaoning Provinces and than Mongolians in terms of international outlook.[17] However, in May 1984 when Hu Yaobang, CCP General Secretary, visited Yanbian on his way back from North Korea, he specifically instructed Yanbian to pursue an open-door policy toward foreign countries for the sake of four-modernizations effort. He also asked Yanbian leaders to establish a memorial hall for the late Chu Tok-hae as a symbol of Korean ethnic achievements; Hu also wrote the name for this hall.

Another potentially serious problem is an emerging generation gap among Koreans in China. A significant proportion of the Koreans in their 50s and older belong to the first generation of immigrants and thus are naturally inclined to retain a strong sense of emotional and cultural attachment to their native homeland. They all have personal memories of Japanese colonial rule, the Korean independence movements, China's pre-Communist reality, and the Korean War experience. As suggested by their attitude toward Sino-Korean sports contests, some Koreans seem to show their primary sentimental attachment to Korea (either North Korea or South Korea) rather than to China. This

161

is in sharp contrast to younger Koreans who were born
and raised in the PRC and were indoctrinated in Maoist
ideology. Unlike the Moslems and Tibetans, there is no
significant religious linkage or psychological
continuity between generations among Koreans. While
the older generation may be anxious to preserve their
ethnically distinct educational and cultural programs
and to transmit their Korean values, customs, and
aspirations to their descendants, the younger
generation is not always able or willing to emulate
their parental model. President Pak Mun-il of Yanbian
University is worried about the "loss of language" (uno
ryusil) among some Korean youth; 10 percent of the
Koreans living in China do not know the Korean
language.[18] The more educated and professional they
are, the more adaptive they become toward the
imperatives of China's integrative forces. This
tendency is particularly evident in China's urban areas
outside Yanbian where the traditional ties among
Koreans are inevitably weakened. It is also bolstered
by the lack of clear physical, religious, and social
distinction between Koreans and Han Chinese and by the
powerful effects of China's Han-centered mass media.

A Korean educator in Liaoning Province says that
"in general, Korean students are relatively serious,
candid, courteous, and rule-abiding. However, a few of
them have an ambiguous concept of fatherland and a
pessimistic view about their ethnic future."[19] Another
Korean scholar in China rhetorically asked: "If the
mass media in Beijing can openly report the return of
overseas Chinese scholars to their "fatherland"

(namely, China), why can't I call Korea my fatherland?"
It is indeed an intensely emotional and politically
sensitive issue among some Koreans in China. In order
to clarify their political socialization and to
forestall any possibility that they might regard Korea
as their fatherland, the very first sentence in the
introductory textbook (Hanyuwen) in the Chinese
language published in Yanbian for Korean students
unequivocally declares that womende zuguo shi zhonghua
renmin gonheguo ("Our fatherland is the People's
Reepublic of China.") Even though the young Koreans in
China are consciously or unconsciously socialized to
accommodate the dominant Han Chinese culture, a large
number of them are apparently confident of their ethnic
identity and cultural heritage and prefer to marry
Korean spouses. They continue to observe Korean social
customs and to favor Korean food--kimchi (pickled
vegetables) and pulgogi (roast beef). Many still live
in traditional Korean houses with thatched-roof and
ondol (heating system). Girls often dress up in
colorful Korean costumes--chima (skirt) and chogori
(coat)--at festivals and special occasions, such as
school picnics, public meetings, and wedding
ceremonies.[20] It is not uncommon even on ordinary days
for Korean women to wear chima and chogori to go to
work (sometimes on bicycles), study, or shop in Yanji
City.

In one of her moving letters written in Korean,
Miss Chang says how happy she was to meet with me. She
states that "the sense of ethnic affinity is a precious
human feeling that can never disappear. It is a basic

morality that transcends state boundaries, gender differences, and generation gaps." She explains that if she marries a non-Korean, she will be permanently ostracized by her family and relatives. While her mother warns that if she has a non-Korean husband, she will never be allowed to enter her home again, her father threatens that he will break her legs in such a case. A senior Korean scientist in Beijing who is married to a Han doctor says that all of their children are registered as ethnic Koreans. He adds that although his children do not speak Korean, they do not mind being called Koreans. Even among those children who have Han Chinese fathers and Korean mothers, there is a modest tendency for them to identify themselves as Koreans not only because they are proud of their partial Korean parentage, but also because they can enjoy the advantages of a minority nationality ranging from educational opportunities and birth control (two children permitted for a minority. couple) to preferences given in a rationing system (for example, more rice for Koreans). One important psychological and practical advantage that Koreans in China have over their counterparts in Japan, the United States, or the Soviet Union is the fact that they have absolutely no compunctions in retaining and using their indigenous Korean names. They see no reason whatsoever to change their family names as a majority of Koreans do in Japan, or to adopt local first names like John Kim or David Hong in the United States or Georgu Kim or Mikhail Pak in the Soviet Union.[21]

Most important, the direction of China's overall political system exerts a fundamental impact on the intellectual and cultural development of all minority nationalities. The central government at Beijing sets a prevailing ideological and political climate, enunciates the pattern of political socialization, and determines the range of educational experimentation or scholarly pursuits among ethnic communities. Despite China's moderate and realistic minority policy, minority nationalities are not free from a lingering feeling of anxiety and apprehension--the unfortunate legacy of the Rectification Movement and the Cultural Revolution. The Korean minority in China is no exception to this system-wide phenomenon, and is subjected to the pressure of Lenin's dictum, "national in form, socialist in content." In order to protect and develop their ethnically-based educational programs, Koreans are compelled to be sensitive and adaptive to the Chinese system--its changing requirements and opportunities. They all hope that China can continue its current minority policy, which is quite favorable and tolerant toward ethnic minorities. For this reason they often express their appreciation to Deng Xiaoping, Hu Yaobang, and Zhao Ziyang, who visited Yanbian in 1983, 1984, and 1980, respectively. For the past 36 years they have learned in a very hard way how to assert their Korean identity in the educational processes without upsetting China's overall national interests. Undoubtedly the success or failure of their educational efforts will determine to a great extent the future status and well-being of the

Korean minority nationality in China. And other minority nationalities in China will continue to observe the Korean case with interest and concern.

NOTES

1. Henry G. Schwarz, "Communist Language Policies," 177.

2. Eight Korean literary persons were Lim Hyo-won, Li Kon-jon, Li Uk, Li Song-hwi, Kim Chol, Kim Chang-gol, Chong Kil-un, and Hwang Pong-ryong. As of 1985 there were 32 Korean members in the Chinese Writers' Association.

3. Interviews with Pak Kyu-chan and Tian Renyong.

4. For Kim Chi-ha, see Yanbian Daxue Xuebao, Number 1 (1983); for Kim Tong-ni, see Arirang, Number 3 (April 1981); and for O Yong-su, see Munhak kwa Yaesul, Number 4 (July-August, 1985).

5. Yonbyon Kyoyuk, Number 3 (1979), 3.

6. New York Times, March 11, 1984.

7. Interview with Li Pyong-hak.

8. Kang Yong-dok, 10-11.

9. Li Hwi-il, "Zongjie minzu," 3.

10. Dreyer, 266.

11. For examples, see Yonbyon Kyoyuk, Number 9 (1982), 22-23.

12. Yonbyon Kyoyuk, Number 12 (1982), 5.

13. Ibid., Number 9 (1982), 21.

14. Ibid., Number 12 (1982), 4.

15. Jilin Ribao, September 18, 1981.

16. Choe Ryong-hak (Cui Longhe), "Yanbiandiqu renkou suzhi yu jingji xiaoyi" [Population Quality and Economic Benefits in the Yanbian Area], in Yanbian Daxue Xuebao (1984, special edition), 165-172.

17. Interview with Kanno Hiroomi, October 1, 1983, Tokyo.

18. Pak Mun-il, "Chungguk yonbyon."

19. Yonbyon Kyoyuk, Number 3 (1982), 7.

20. For the preservation of Korean social customs in China, see Zhongguo shaoshuminzu, 43-56, Renmin Ribao, September 21, 1981 and October 28, 1983, and Minzu Huabao, September 1982.

21. For the problems faced by Koreans in Japan, see Changsoo Lee and George De Vos, Koreans in Japan: Ethnic Conflict and Accommodation (Berkeley: University of California Press, 1981).